Death of a Mother

Daughters' Stories

Edited by
Rosa Ainley

An Imprint of HarperCollins*Publishers*

Pandora
An Imprint of HarperCollins*Publishers*
77–85 Fulham Palace Road,
Hammersmith, London W6 8JB
1160 Battery Street,
San Francisco, California 94111–1213

Published by Pandora 1994
10 9 8 7 6 5 4 3 2 1

© Rosa Ainley 1994

Rosa Ainley asserts the moral right to
be identified as the author of this work

A catalogue record for this book
is available from the British Library

ISBN 0 04 440928 1

Printed in Great Britain by
HarperCollinsManufacturing Glasgow

For Helena

Contents

Preface

My mother is dead.
Four simple words, but what an ocean of meaning lies beneath them. Not a simple stream flowing in one direction, but a vast ocean of hidden depths, fierce undercurrents, gentle eddies and mountainous, crashing waves – knowing and not knowing, presence and absence, love and hate, acceptance and rejection, joy and bitterness, guilt and salvation, shame and glory.

Whether your mother is alive and with you, or dead, or absent and unknown, the way you see her – in actuality, memory or fantasy – is central to how you see yourself and your life. How you see her and respond to her is never simple.

'My mother' – a looming, powerful giant and an ordinary woman.

'Is dead' – she who is immortal is no more.

When in the course of conversation I say, 'My mother is dead' my listeners are not surprised. I'm sixty-three, so my mother is likely to be dead. To say these words when you're a child or a young woman is to invite danger. Will your listeners ignore what you say, or become over solicitous, or seek to satisfy their curiosity by asking wounding questions? After all, mothers shouldn't die until they're old. That's their duty.

However, no matter how old you get, saying these words is not easy. My aunt at ninety-four prefers to think of her mother, dead for half a century, as still living in the family home in the Australian bush. My aunt is not senile. She just prefers occasionally to think of herself as being at home with her mother and not as being in her efficient and boring nursing home. For daughters (and sons), mothers might die but they never disappear.

If your mother dies when she is old people murmur, 'She had a good life,' or 'It's a blessed release' and hope that you will 'take it well', that is, not get upset in front of them. If your mother dies when she's young people withdraw from you in embarrassment. The death not only reminds them of their own and their mothers' death but it also threatens their sentimental belief that this is a Just World where goodness is rewarded and badness punished. Death shows us that life is unfair, a matter of chance, and that you can't keep yourself safe by being good.

What could be more unfair than your mother dying when you're a child? Rather than feel the pain of pity, people turn away from a child's grief and say, 'Children soon get over it. Children forget.'

But children don't forget. No matter how old you become, you don't forget your childhood. Some people say they don't remember their childhood, but usually what they are doing is keeping themselves so busy attending to the present and the future that they don't have time to remember. When friends and relatives reminisce such people do remember their past, unless what is forgotten is too painful to remember.

Forgetting or remembering, to say to yourself, 'My mother is dead' is always a strange experience. Yes, you've grown up now. You know that everyone dies, and then you think, 'But not my mother.'

Mother must not die. While she is alive you cannot be old. You cannot be alone. You have a home to go to, even if you don't want to be there.

Your mother secures your identity, and what is your identity but your life story, your past, your present and your future?

Your mother creates your life story and weaves it into the vast web of life stories of human existence. If your mother vanishes before she has done this and no one else undertakes the task you become a rootless, lonely wanderer in the world where everyone else seems to have a family and a proper past. In her piece *Case Notes*, Rachel Williams, whose mother had vanished when she was ten and who was then taken into foster care, writes,

> In each new placement I was expected to forget the past and make a new start. Foster families related to each other through their shared histories and experiences. They showed me photographs and reminisced about their lives. Cut off from my own roots, I sat smiling stupidly, deeply ashamed of a disjointed past I did not understand and could not speak of.

Growing up means learning to look after yourself. How can you learn to do this? Your mother in caring for you shows you how to care for yourself. But what if she isn't there to show you this? Rachel Williams, in therapy to turn depression into mourning, says to her absent mother,

> My longing to be with you does not fade, nor my deep sorrow that you could not nurture me, that you are

not here. It is not easy to nurture myself when I am so ambivalent about my own life.

Your mother secures your future by showing you what you will, in part, become. To be yourself you rebel against your mother, yet your opposing stance contains what it opposes. I became a resolute optimist to protect myself from my mother's profound pessimism, and thus I know how to be pessimistic, and I sometimes am, but fortunately without my mother's self-absorbed bitterness.

Zelda Curtis made a similar discovery. In *Be 'Someone'* she writes,

> I understand how like her I really am, and in a way it has always frightened me. Yet I can think of ways in which I do hope I am like her. After her death I would find myself looking into the mirror to find my mother's face staring back at me. I found myself examining my actions for signs of her in me, and finding them. I found myself checking my relationships with my daughters – and wondering.

What comes through in all the voices in this book telling of the death of their mothers are the two opposing currents in the ocean of meaning underlying 'My mother is dead.' These currents are the longing for the mother's love and the fear of her power. The love is often mixed with anger at her inadequacy and her absence. The fear is often the fear called guilt.

Mothers never die. They live on inside us and we can find peace only when we can resolve the conflict between the fear they inspire and their love. Zelda Curtis writes,

> Death is real, but I have never believed in it as a parting. My mother is within me and in all my actions. I can see her face in mine and in my mind I can hear her

voice and can giggle at some of her funny sayings.
'Aren't you lucky, Zelda,' she said when my first daughter was born, 'to have a mother who has had children!'
But I also hear some of her less wise sayings coming out of my own mouth sometimes. It worries me.
My guilt is now assuaged. My anger has gone and time takes away some of the pain. Perhaps I can carry my mother within me more comfortably now, with greater understanding and compassion.

To grow up you have to outgrow your mother. As long as you experience her as enveloping you, holding you in the conflicts of power and fear, knowing and not knowing, presence and absence, love and hate, acceptance and rejection, joy and bitterness, guilt and salvation, shame and glory, you cannot become what you might be.

Everything that we invest with meaning comes to us in the form of the story. The story is the basic form in which we think. We know and tell stories. To know we must listen and tell.

To outgrow your mother and become what you can be, you need to tell the story of you and your mother and listen to others tell theirs. Some people, mindful of the Fifth Commandment, 'Honour thy father and mother so that thy days shall be long in the land,' fear to tell their story even to themselves and so remain trapped as a child in their mother's presence.

Hearing others tell their story can give us the courage to tell our own. Through such telling your mother can become an ordinary person and a special, eternal friend.

Dorothy Rowe
August, 1994

Acknowledgements

'A Hard Death' and 'Of Grief' are reprinted from
Collected Poems (1930–1993) by May Sarton, by permission of W.W. Norton & Company, Inc., ©1993, 1988,
1984, 1974 by May Sarton.

'Autumn 1980' also appears in *The Hang-Glider's Daughter*, Onlywomen Press, 1990, and in *Assumptions*,
Knopf, N.Y., 1985.

'Mother' also appears in *Assumptions*.

Introduction

That hour began my wanderings. Not so much in geography, but in time.
Then not so much in time as in spirit.

Dust Tracks on a Road – Zora Neale Hurston

Everyone has a mother and everyone dies – these are two certainties in our lives. The importance and complexity of both elements – mother and death – have conspired to silence many of the women who've experienced the death of their mothers, and stop others from wanting to know about it. It's easy to see why reactions to the idea of this anthology have often been less than positive. It's a frightening prospect: most daughters will see their mothers die.

Death of a Mother is an effort to make discussion possible, to allow death back into life, and to focus on the particular meanings of a mother's death. Many women write in the book of there being nothing left between them and old age once their mothers have died; nothing between them and their own death, no last resort, no safety net – no mother. The death of a mother can mean the end of all possibilities for mutual understanding, reconciliation or discovery, but paradoxically it may also mean the unleashing of a daughter's capacity for exploring and analysing that relationship. It's important to make clear that this unravelling of the experience is no less a necessity for women who didn't have 'good' relationships with their mothers, who didn't like their mothers or who, for whatever reason, felt a huge relief at the death. Experiencing death always involves some re-evaluation of life, and, alongside the more personal feelings of bereavement, dwelling on the life of someone now dead and your own life without her is often intertwined with the shock of facing up to mortality.

The mother-daughter relationship is particular, important – but it doesn't exist apart from other relationships (family and otherwise), and quite a lot of the works in this book also concern themselves with fathers, dead and alive. How we feel about our fathers is no less worthy of attention. I wanted to demonstrate that a mother's death reverberates through her daughter's life, to document the effects on other family relationships (of the biological, adoptive and hand-picked variety), and on friendships, on attitudes and behaviour towards lovers, on who our lovers might be.

Although there have been a number of books published on the relationship between women and their mothers – books of letters, experiential/confessional writing, feminist scholarship – about the death of a mother there is a strictly limited choice. What little there is (see booklist) tends to be written for professionals, for those dealing with 'The Bereaved'. In many different cultures, a myriad of taboos inhibit talk about death, especially where children are concerned. I know, for instance, that during the compilation of this book at least three women discovered details surrounding their mothers' deaths they hadn't known before. Secrets have long lives.

Not that everyone suffers from uncontrollable and/or unexpressed grief when their mother dies – some of us even make jokes about it. But no one should pretend it's of only minor importance. Ordinary and extraordinary, it is an experience that has to be talked about. I think particularly here of children – many of those writing in this book whose mothers died when they were young told lies about it because they were (made to feel) ashamed of how their mother had died, or simply because she was dead, and they easily picked up the signs telling them this wasn't something anyone wanted to talk about much.

Given the lack of opportunity for anyone to express feelings, from the expected first grief to the less acceptable longer-term reactions including anger, dislike, relief and confusion, it isn't surprising that therapy often appears as a solution or necessity in the pieces in this anthology. Some of the contributors have found it useful in understanding the impact of the experience on their lives, and in living with the death of a figure so powerful. Others find it unnecessary; still others talk of surviving both the onslaught of death *and* that of therapy. There's a whole industry around bereavement counselling, too, which is of course a very different thing, and there are attendant limitations to it. Briefly, there is a danger in that it can become too bound by specific textbook patterns of bereavement, as Valerie Smith notes in *An Ordinary Experience*. If death and grief were not forced into a position of such silent partnership in our lives, would there be any need for bereavement counselling?

This anthology never set out to be any kind of 'How to' guide, although it will be useful in that way to counsellors and therapists. As well as a short booklist there is, at the back of the book, a piece on organising a funeral and a list of relevant organisations. Neither was *Death of a Mother* conceived as definitive, nor as an attempt to include every variable, each cause of death, each ritual, each reaction. Rather, it's meant to offer an exploration, from over thirty different perspectives, of some of the many aspects of the death of a mother, from those most clearly linked to the death to those seemingly unconnected with it.

A healthy society should be able to accept and deal with death. The first book I got hold of about childhood, separation and death (over twenty years *after* I'd become a suitable subject for such a tome) told me, in no uncertain terms, that children whose mothers had died were more likely to grow up to be alcoholic, die by suicide and be unable to form worthwhile relationships. While that kind of pathologising of grief and loss has thankfully fallen out of favour, its reverberations have far-reaching effects, both in terms of self-image and attitudes from the medical and support professions. And still we are afraid to talk too much, too long about death.

- I don't want to talk of this anymore.
- Then it will always be a nightmare.

In the Skin of the Lion – Michael Ondaatje

'Breaking silences' is a phrase so over-used that it's probably been to cliché and back by now; I hope so, because that's what this book does. I want to see death recognised ('resurrected' is the word I really want to use here) in life, as an everyday part of the journey, rather than the 'Horror & Tragedy', tabloid style, or the schmaltz of Hollywood.

To write about your mother being dead can be a difficult and painful process. Many women who originally wanted to write for this book either didn't or couldn't. Many found it too upsetting, thought the idea of uncovering feelings too daunting, or were put off by the prospect of their family's reactions. Writing about death is made even harder by this – imagine then the prohibitions over which we stumble and also discover in ourselves, when the writer wants to express relief, or hatred, or glee. It's an act of bravery to speak ill of the dead. The reticence we experience in talking about death and dying makes grief harder to express, and harder to be accepted. Fear and lack of information can easily lead to depression and passivity. There are so many reasons against the appearance of this book. Families, fear, ritual. Some of the contributors celebrate, but many more used their space to explore, to grieve.

The lack, in many cultures, of rituals around death which could possibly ease the processes of both dying and grieving compounds the problems all of us face. A short cremation ceremony, for instance, does not count as an open, ritualised display of grief, and therefore its usefulness to the living is strictly limited – some of the pieces mention its function as that of offering something that needs to be organised, that must be concentrated on shortly after the death. As the section on 'Planning a funeral' notes, a more sensitively evolved ritual could have a use beyond 'getting you through the first difficult days', could indeed be structured so that support and expression were not limited to the (short) period immediately following the death.

Writing of death may be painful, but ultimately it is positive because all of us – including the women whose work could not be included in this collection – have, literally, survived to tell the tale. Writing may be a part of a healing process, to own your experience and feelings and recognise them as worthy of publication. These pieces display differing levels of rawness, self-protection, exposure, both in the events related and the forms and methods chosen to relate them. Experience and writing shared equal importance in the selection procedure.

In compiling *Death of a Mother* I looked for a diversity in form and approach as well as experience, for contributions from women whose mothers had died recently and long ago, after long illnesses and suddenly; women who had close and difficult relationships with their mothers, foster-mothers, adoptive mothers. I wanted to reveal that there is no homogeneous identity amongst women whose mothers are dead – like any other group of women, a variety of cultural, social and economic factors affect our relationships with our mothers, with death and how we deal (or not) with these events.

Submissions came in the form of letters, short stories, diaries, essays, personal and more theoretical accounts. There is very little fiction. Most of the pieces included are personal accounts, the small amount of fiction reflecting the proportion I received. This may follow a more general pattern in women's writing: testimony first, fiction later. It's also notable that many of the contributions are not straightforward chronological narratives – how, when telling your own story, do you decide what to include, where to stop, how to effect an ending? Formulating an ending is an added complication in a difficult process, an experience that's constantly in progress, which often contains no final resolution in your own life. Some of the endings therefore have a feeling of temporariness; chapter endings rather than final conclusions. Endings are often literally ones that each author has constructed; perhaps we do write fiction after all.

There are similarities and repetitions within the diversity of experience – concern about how much we resemble our mothers, physically or otherwise, mothers as ghosts, benevolent or not, in our lives, the hurt of being denied information, the euphemism of the hospital side ward, the inability (through pressure of work and embarrassment rather than anything more sinister) of many professionals to ease the death or the bereavement. Much of the material is about mothers as a presence in our lives, as well as an absence. Many of the writers relate their mother dying to their own feelings about motherhood. Certainly there's a whole clutch of clichés – about births easing deaths, about the two-way nature of nurturing, about the process of endings and renewal, about mothers letting their daughters grow up only when the daughters become mothers themselves – to attest to the importance of the subject.

> A hemisphere
> away from understanding where you are,
> mourning your lost words, I am at a loss
> for words to name what my loss of you is,
> what it will be, or even what it was.

> 'Against Silence' – Marilyn Hacker

For similar reasons some of the contributions have a disjointed, episodic structure and tone, rather than being smooth and seamless narratives. They are journeys, not arrivals or departures – even at the point of ultimate ending, the final departure, the writing in this book is really about beginnings. Often the pieces reflect journeys through memory and imagination where good-byes are said, leave taken, because opportunities were not given or taken in life.

I have chosen pieces that, I think, best express different aspects of the experience of our mothers dying – the death itself, the funeral and other surrounding ceremonies and rituals, the rest of our lives, and how this is affected depending on when in your life it happens. Death and children are the stuff of sentiment indeed, but many adults have felt themselves transported back to childhood at the death of a parent, while others have found release and relief from more or less tangible parental limitation.

As the editor I've sometimes been quite literally overwhelmed by the material, which has been extremely welcome – providing me, finally, with a means to talk about my mother to people who won't change the subject, squirm around, or shut me up with sympathy. But also, the 'there's going to be a book about it' mentality has lead to a strange new validity – it's never before been so acceptable, so well received, to discuss your mother being dead. My cynical reservations aside, to assert that validity had been one of the major aims behind the publication of *Death of a Mother*. At times it was unwanted, becoming too much for me to deal with and forcing me to recognise what I had involved myself in, and to wonder what the cost to myself was going to be.

For instance, during the time when I was receiving a lot of submissions for the book, the *Guardian* carried an article about children whose parents had gone to fight in the Gulf War. The article began, 'For a child the loss of a parent is a trauma that will haunt him for life. The loss of two parents is a catastrophe.' The same day I was in a shop when I overheard part of a radio phone-in where a woman was talking about her dead father. 'I thought if I made myself self-sufficient I'd get over it,' she was saying. I had to walk out of the shop. The article made me want to give up on the book entirely, take to my bed, and give in to my destiny as a living trauma zone. The woman on the radio elicited an opposing response: to publish the book immediately, so that both she and the radio doctor who was dealing with her call could read it. So that she would stop saying things that I used to say, and so that I wouldn't have to walk out of my local shop because I felt so haunted and exposed. Both incidents made me want to transmute into some remarkably successful, healed, whole role model (although I'm not sure what this might involve). Simultaneously magnifying and contradicting my experience of working on the anthology, these two occurrences exposed some very tender spots about the whole thing, as well as the importance of continuing with it.

The process of compiling and selecting the pieces for *Death of a Mother* has been quite unusual in the amount of contact and confidences I've had with contributors: these were always valuable and often upsetting. The recognition and affirmation I've received have been priceless to me – that's what I want the experience of reading this book to be for others, too.

This book is, then, for everyone with or without a mother. I hope it will be useful to those whose mothers are dead, that the affirmation of shared experience will empower them. I hope it will enable those whose mothers are still alive to look clearly at this almost inevitable experience, and thereby purge some of the fear, to make it ordinary indeed. The more we talk about death the less fearful and isolating bereavement will become, and the more prepared we will be for the shock, when it comes.

As long as they were alive we were always someone's children, someone's daughter. Could there be a world without her mother? Of course there could be, there would be, there already was, as there would be a world without herself. That she could easily imagine. No ghost would remain, no chair would stay empty, no space open up; only a small flame left in the kitchen.

Years from Now – Gary Glickman

About the Authors

Rosa Ainley
is North London born and bred (a lifestyle seriously disrupted by her parents' dying) and has now moved eastwards.

Susan Ardill
returned to live in Sydney in 1992, where she has been working as a documentary producer for Film Australia.

Leland Bardwell
was born in India. Grew up in Co. Kildare. Has six grown-up children. Now lives in Co. Monaghan. Has published four novels, three collections of poems, three stage plays, several radio plays for the BBC and RTE, and a collection of short stories. Most recent publication is a book of poems, *Dostoevsky's Grave* (Dedalus, 1991). In progress, a fourth collection of poems, plays and a novel.

Julie Bellian
was born in Toronto, Canada, in 1959. Moved to London at nineteen and studied art, then took a degree in Humanities and finally an MA in Women's Studies. Throughout this

time, she travelled in Europe and the Middle East, and worked in Italy. Now *en route* to the west coast of Canada, carrying her love of dance, people, and everything wild, with a new vision of creativity and community.

Suzanne Bosworth
has wanted to write since the age of seven. She is now a published writer of social issues, satire and short stories, and is active in Green politics and in human and animal rights movements.

Gail Chester
was born in 1951 into an orthodox Jewish family, and is now a born-again atheist. An active feminist for more than half her life, she has edited a number of books including *In Other Words: Writing as a Feminist* (with Sigride Nielsen) and *Feminism and Censorship: the current debate* (with Julienne Dickey). The present article is part of a collection which would have been written straight after her mother's death, had she not immediately got pregnant. Three years and a young son uncannily like his grandmother later, she is now back at her desk.

Norma Cohen
is movement-trained and has worked in theatre/TV and on radio as an actress, choreographer and director. Journalism on dance/TIE/disability includes features for *The Guardian*, *Yorkshire Post*, *Dance and Dancers* and *Therapy Weekly*. She was *City Limits'* Health Editor and is the *Times Educational Supplement*'s Dance Editor. Comic monologues and short story *The Last Supper* have been broadcast on BBC Radio 4. Publications include *Theatre Works: a guide to working in the theatre* (National Press), and *Women and Fitness* and *Out of Focus* (The Women's Press).

She is completing a stage play, *Sink or Swim* and has returned to performing. She has a sixteen-year-old daughter.

Shirley P. Cooper

has been in England for twenty-eight years and has had numerous addresses, banks and occupations. Besides rearing her ten-year-old daughter, Joanne, who also writes, she ran three direct-selling businesses. She retired from teaching in 1989 to renovate her house and publish the teaching packs, articles, stories and poems she has written. She is a member of Burbury Creative Writers' Circle, which is part of the Federation of Worker Writers and Community Publishers.

Zelda Curtis

was born 1923 in Hackney. After a grammar school education she served during the Second World War in the WAAF, then came marriage and the birth of her two daughters. Her career spanned work in Unity Theatre; at *Labour Monthly*, *Morning Star* and *East End News*; at War on Want. Her main interest now is campaigning for Older Women's issues and she is a member of AGLOW – Association of Greater London Older Women.

Lynden Easterbrook

worked for Women's Aid for ten years. She now works as a Counsellor and Education Social Worker. She lives in Derbyshire where she enjoys walking, running and photography.

Rahila Gupta

is a freelance writer and journalist; she also works part-time as a publications officer. She is a member of the Asian Women Writers Collective and of Southall Black Sisters.

Marilyn Hacker
is the author of nine books, including *Winter Numbers* and *Selected Poems 1965–1990*, both published by W. W. Norton, 1994. *Love, Death, and the Changing of the Seasons* and *The Hang-Glider's Daughter* were published in Great Britain by Onlywomen Press. From 1990 through 1994, she was editor of *The Kenyon Review*. She divides her time between New York and Paris.

Caroline Halliday
For those who know the terror and the grief: this writing more than any is a part of her own body. Honour it. That's how it seems in writing about death and grief... the terror she has felt and the few bits of comfort. It is only two years since her mother died, and she is growing through to accept, though perhaps not yet to deal with the deep loneliness... and to live again. What else is in her life? Her wonderful daughter, of course... and they are moving transThames, the biggest move for eighteen years... this is creative... she deals with separation, change, stress, and hopefulness... no writing, yet!

Emma Hindley
is in her thirties, lives in Hackney, makes documentary films and comes from a large family.

Jo Hughes
was born in Swansea in 1956. She studied art and design at Swansea and Ealing and has worked for many magazines including *Spare Rib*, *Women's Review*, *City Limits* and *Everywoman*. She lives in London with her four-year-old daughter.

Margaret Jacobs
lives in Melbourne, Australia. She has worked in teaching, community radio, government departments and for a group of people with intellectual disabilities. Recently she has been involved with Women in Black, a vigil movement calling for Israeli withdrawal from the Occupied Territories. She is editing a book her mother wrote about her life in pre-war Germany.

Barbara James
was born in Canada and is now experiencing the decline of civilisation in London where she works in Women's Health and the British Library.

Frances Kenton
is a Novacastrian interested in poetry, printmaking and allotments.

Helen Pausacker
was born in Australia in 1954. She works part-time in a variety of office jobs. Helen is a keen cyclist and has been active in mixed gay movement activities for over ten years.

Jill Posener
was born 1953 and is currently living in San Francisco with lover/partner Susie and a menagerie of dogs and cats. A photo-journalist, her two books of political graffiti photos, *Spray it Loud* and *Louder than Words*, were both published by Pandora. She has contributed to anthologies like *Stolen Glances* and *Dagger* and has been published in magazines and newspapers as varied as the *New York Times* and the *Village Voice*.

Mandy Rose
lives in London. She works for the BBC as co-producer of the Video Nation project.

Sally St Clair
is a mother and writer. Born in south-east London and educated at a GPDST school. On leaving, she had a brief spell at Art School but left there to concentrate on motherhood. Between 1984 and 1992 she studied science and took a degree in Biology with Education at York University, where she learned that she did not much like the academic world.

May Sarton
was born in Belgium in 1912, her father the historian of science George Sarton, her mother, Mabel Elwes, an English artist and designer. She has published sixteen novels, twelve books of poetry, nine journals and memoirs. She lives in York, Maine in a house by the sea with a Himalayan cat called Pierrot.

Robyn Selman
was born 1959, has published poems most recently in *Ploughshares*, *Conditions*, *Puerto Del Sol* and *Best American Poetry, 1991*. Her criticism has appeared in *The Village Voice* and *The Nation*. She lives and works in New York City.

Shireen Sheikh
is a pseudonym. *The Other Mother* is a 'faction', part fact, part fiction.

Valerie Smith
is in her fifties, married with two grown-up daughters. She was born in London and grew up in Hounslow, but has been

living in Yorkshire for twenty-five years. She started her working life as a medical laboratory technician, and then changed direction in her thirties, studying for an external degree in English literature and now works as a part-time tutor in adult and higher education.

Carol Tilbury
is in her mid-forties, a teacher living and working in Hackney. She has two teenage daughters who, like their grandmother, both love to dance.

Rachel Williams
is forty-seven and lives in Bristol. She is a survivor of the 'care' system and the psychiatric system. Currently, she is a student on a social work course.

An Ordinary Experience

Valerie Smith

I expected to be grief-stricken when my mother died, but instead I felt as though someone had hit me over the head with a club, or as if I had a bad dose of flu. I had not anticipated that bereavement would be so literally a blow. I am nearly fifty, but this was my first close encounter with death. My mother died, after a single night's illness, of a pulmonary embolism, a sudden but not unexpected end. My father coped alone with the messy business of her dying, and the next day the widely-scattered family gathered to support him in his solitude and grief. At night the visitors returned to their own homes, and I stayed to keep him company.

My father and I kept the household routine going, talked to visitors, answered the phone and waited for the funeral. On the third night, as I lay awake, a thought came unbidden into my head – 'Now she will not be able to be unkind to me any more.'

This was so painful that I could hardly bear it. I decided that if I shut this off it would fester; I had to think it out and see what happened.

So I did, and it got worse and worse. All around me, people were talking about what a good woman my mother was

– difficult at times, yes – but how she always did her duty, how she had been a mother to her grandchildren through years of family crisis. 'What about me?' I raged in my head. 'What sort of a mother was she to me? Her idea of support was to brace me with a cold shower of criticism. When did she ever praise me or my achievements?'

I stayed for three weeks, and then I had to go home to my own work, my own family. The anger persisted. I spent a whole evening weeping, remembering a time when she had made me wear a particularly horrible version of the school uniform – for no real reason that I could understand unless she thought that adversity was good for the spirit; I wept for hours about an indignity that had ended more than thirty years before. I began to think that, if not mad, I must certainly be bad. It was time to do something about it.

In the usual way of academics, I went to the library and read every book I could find on the subject of bereavement. I dropped my current research and read voraciously for weeks on end. My exploration branched out into books on mothers and daughters, and my file of notes grew thicker and thicker. After about six weeks I stopped this gluttonous reading, picked up and finished my earlier project, and returned, more calmly, to complete the bereavement study.

I was amazed that there was so little relevant material available. The near-universal experience of bereavement by the death of a parent in adulthood – a major event in anyone's life – is almost unstudied. It appears to be regarded as so 'natural' as to be unworthy of research. Other such changes – puberty, marriage – are studied extensively, but the death of a mother or father, which shifts one's whole pattern of relationships, goes all but unremarked.

The topics of death, dying and bereavement have only been studied fully in recent years, and certain names such as C. M. Parkes and Elisabeth Kübler-Ross recur again and again in the literature. Their research grew out of clinical work with the dying, or with those suffering psychological distress after bereavement, and so the model of illness/patient/professional diagnosis and care is imposed upon the experience. (One might draw parallels with the medicalisation of childbirth.) Published studies concentrate on three areas: death of a young child, death by sudden accident, and death of a spouse. We now expect all our children to live and be healthy; we expect to live to old age ourselves. Any reversal of these expectations is obviously exceedingly painful, and quite different from my own experience. My bereavement has more in common with that suffered by those who have lived together for fifty years, and who *must* expect one of the partners to die first. So I read about bereavement caused by the death of a spouse, and searched for material that dealt with adult children and elderly parents; getting interested, I looked for mention of reactions to the death of friends or lovers or colleagues, of uncles, cousins, aunts, instead of the intimate dyads of husband/wife, parent/child.

I am not a sociologist or a psychologist, and to my amateur eyes the research seemed at times full of holes. Much of the work on spouse bereavement was in fact a study of widows; and the distress and difficulty they encountered would be felt by any woman suddenly required to live on a reduced income, to run a household and perhaps to bring up a family alone. The extra help that widowers receive from family and friends was taken for granted.

All the studies required voluntary co-operation, and none achieved more than a 50 per cent response from those invited to take part. Among the respondents, certain elements of grief were indeed present over and over again.

The first stage of grief is represented as a state of shock, a great blow, a numbing experience; the mind struggles to accept that the death has actually happened, is irrevocable.

As it sinks in, the real grieving begins, and the sense of irreparable loss results in tears and misery. At the same time, anger and guilt are felt: Why did you leave me? Why didn't I do more for you when you were alive? Why didn't the doctors try harder to save you? Gradually, as time passes, and with the help of family and the support of family and friends, this stage gives way to a quieter acceptance of loss. Memories become less painful, and can be explored more fully; eventually, a new life is built up again. This sequence of grieving is described repeatedly: but it is also validated by its replication in handbooks for those counselling the bereaved. I searched in vain for references to anger directed *at* the dead person, or to feelings of liberation felt *by* the bereaved. But what about the people who did not respond? Were their feelings as 'inappropriate' as my own? The interviewers shied away from distressing the bereaved, and when negative feelings *were* reported, the researchers seemed reluctant to believe the speaker. It is as though the research itself is spellbound by the British cultural tradition that one does not 'speak ill of the dead', especially of those whose death is recent.

Eventually I unearthed some references to anger and guilt. In *Totem and Taboo* Freud discusses hostility to the dead, saying that this is expressed much more openly in primitive societies; but he does not discuss why attitudes have changed. Most modern writers say that hostility to the dead is redirected, either towards the self or towards the professional carers. Beverly Raphael, following Freud and Bowlby, relates anger to separation anxiety, and considers that anger may be most pronounced when the bereaved had an intense or even infantile dependence on the deceased.

This made quite a lot of sense to me: my mother had a powerful personality and continued to influence me long after I had married and moved two hundred miles away. Part of my rage is almost comic in origin: we have been engaged for the whole of our lives in a battle to have the last word in any argument, and now, by her death, she has made sure of the truly final last word. She has won. In the years before her death, we had reached a more amicable relationship, 'agreeing to disagree' about contentious issues; I thought we had reached a mature understanding of our differences. My anger after her death showed that this did not run very deep, that part of me still yearned for that 'infinitely healing conversation with her' which Adrienne Rich has called 'the unhealed child's fantasies'.

My reading about mothers and daughters – until recent years another neglected area of psychological study, especially in studies of adult women and their mothers – led me to see how much of our conflict had been caused by the powerful ideology of motherhood. My mother thought it natural that a woman's whole life should be centred round husband, home and family. Although she went out to work in various part-time jobs, as have all the women in my family, such work was seen as secondary to the needs of husband and children.

In response to her good mothering, I was expected to be the good daughter: but she defined the good daughter as one who reproduced her own qualities, and any differing from her own standards caused trouble. My reading showed me how much this situation was the creation of particular historical forces: at another time we might have been allies instead of rivals, or our strong personalities would have been diffused among a larger household group. The historical analysis made me feel more hopeful: the situation need not be perpetuated. I had found very painful the idea that my own daughters would greet my death with feelings of rage, relief and liberation. But I do not want to join the chorus of mother-blaming: I am a mother myself.

In recent years, psychologists have become more interest-

ed in whole-life studies, looking at the entire span of a
human life; they are beginning to discuss adult bereavement, and the relationships between adult children and
elderly parents. However, I still found that academic studies
seemed to ignore feelings and emotional responses, and that
I had to go to more literary sources for any understanding of
the underlying relationships. I have said that few bereavement studies take into account 'inappropriate' negative feelings; almost none describes any positive responses, except
the common phrase 'a happy release' when the deceased had
suffered much pain and ill-health. In anecdotal sources,
bereaved middle-aged children share my feelings of liberation into true adulthood; but such feelings of liberation are
not touched on in academic works.

I found one (1965) study by the anthropologist Geoffrey
Gorer which dealt much more fully with ordinary bereavement, and which covered a wide range of relationships. I
wish that there were more studies along these lines, to show
reactions to bereavement in a more representative sample of
society, and to get away from the clinical model whereby
grief is seen as an illness. I would like works on grief to take
account of the loss that is felt on the death of friends, or colleagues at work, or a long-standing lover. We have no social
mechanism for expressing mourning in these bereavements
outside the family – and yet a next-door neighbour can be a
more important person in everyday life, can be more loved
and valued, than a blood relation seen only once a year.

I would like to see research that asks questions about rage
and anger, about the forbidden feelings, the unacceptable
responses to death and bereavement. In learning to cope
with the death of a parent, we begin to face the reality of our
own mortality. It would have helped me to understand the
situation better if I had been able to find fuller, more truth-
ful accounts of the experience of mid-life bereavement. I

would have felt less guilty, less ashamed. Now that time has passed, I have calmed down. I am able, in John Hinton's words, to mourn my mother sincerely 'for the imperfect person she more truly was'.

New Grey Coat

Leland Bardwell

I hated my mother. My mother hated me. Simple. No subtleties about it. I was the third child. She hoped for a boy. I was a girl. She said I was ugly. I was. I was moon-faced. A big head. Had probably hurt her coming out although she never told me that.

We had big rows. Screaming rows. I tried to kill her with a pitchfork. I thought she was stupid. When she got the first cancer I put on a long stripy dress and looked at myself in the mirror. I flattened out my hair and went to see her in the hospital. She said: 'Take off that dress.' I was nine then. I went home and flirted with a tenor from the Gilbert and Sullivan chorus.

She got the second cancer. I was sixteen. I gave her a sixth of a grain of morphine every four hours. She asked me to kill her. I didn't.

My mother was an eccentric who loved my father and my sister and my brother.

She had a horrible mother too.

I hated my grandmother.

She was an old square-shaped woman. Always wore black. Black as a bat, she was. Always angry-faced. I was terrified of her.

My mother couldn't put her hand on her pelvis.

My mother and father slept in different beds.

I'm sure she never had an orgasm.

My mother was dreadfully repressed. She wanted to be a painter. She painted. Quite well. She had a friend called Kitty Lloyd. They went on painting holidays together. Kitty Lloyd wanted to paint my picture but my mother said I was too ugly. Not worth painting. I wanted her to do my side face so as not to paint my moon-front. She did. My mother tore it up. I thought I didn't look too bad. I wrote 'love' on the blotting paper. She beat me. Threatened to tell my grandmother.

She lived for a year with my injections. I played with the syringe. Two days before she died my father got a real nurse. Two real nurses. Night nurse and day nurse. I got a sore throat. I also got a new grey coat. I was glad she was dead.

My sister and my father cried. In the church, that was. We had coffee in the silver coffee-pot. It tasted good. It was a cold February day. I felt light as a jenny-wren. I was an egotistical brat.

Case Notes

In memory of my mother, Betty Florence
Born: October 19th, 1922. Died: February 12th, 1963.

I was separated from you when I was ten. My brother was nine and my sister eight. You said we were going away for a fortnight to a special holiday home for children. I did not want to go. A Children's Officer collected us all in her car and took us to a court, then to a reception centre. You left us there. It was an institutional place of rules and regulations, marching in single file, boys sleeping upstairs and girls down. There was no room for questions or tears. That first night I felt betrayed and terrified I would never see you or my brother again. When Sir and Matron sent us out to play in the grounds next day, we climbed a monkey tree and sat in its branches trying to figure out what was going on. We reckoned you were being kept prisoner somewhere in the building and that our family was being punished for something bad we had done. We did not understand that we had been taken into care. You visited us and said as soon as you found another house we would all be together again. I was afraid to ask what was wrong with the home we once shared. Months went by. We were split up and fostered out. They said it was temporary.

'Foster' is a soft, comforting word that means to nourish, to cherish. But foster-care was a bleak and neglectful reality. Foster-care was punishment. I did not want it, I wanted to go home. No one explained why I could not go home. The not knowing was painful and confusing. I was given board and lodging and little else. No one helped me sort out my feelings. I felt unloved and unwanted and had no sense of belonging, an outsider in other people's families. When people asked why I was fostered, I could find no explanation and felt ashamed and humiliated. I grieved inwardly and got stuck in an autistic state of rageful mourning for you. You never visited any of my foster homes because you were not allowed to and I wondered what you had done that was so terrible. Once or twice a year there were visiting days when you took all three of us to the cinema and out to tea. I clung tightly to your presence. Leaving you at a street corner near my foster home, not knowing if or when I would see you again, was more painful to me than being separated from you by death. A frozen smile hid my intense feelings of terror, sadness and loss.

As a foster-child I was expected to fit in, behave and be grateful. I tried hard to conform in the hope that if I was good you might apply to have me back home, but my suppressed pain and anger found expression in behaviour that was unacceptable to foster-parents. They rejected me for not giving affection, not co-operating, not being happy. I was moved erratically from placement to placement and blamed for being broken and silent. I never knew what the Children's Officer told foster-parents about me and why I had been moved, but I was sure it must be bad. In each new placement I was expected to forget the past and make a new start. Foster-families related to each other through their shared histories and experiences. They showed me photographs and reminisced about their lives. Cut off from my own roots, I sat smiling stupidly, deeply ashamed of a disjointed past I did not understand and could not speak of. I withdrew into lonely longing and waiting for the day when I would go home. Often I wished you were dead so that I could be a respectable orphan.

You died when I was sixteen and in my third foster home. My foster-mother was in hospital having her fourth child. My foster-father informed me late at night that you had died, probably from a brain haemorrhage, and sent me to bed. I was upset that the Children's Officer, my only link with you, did not call and tell me. Upstairs I smoked a cigarette with my foster-sister and climbed into bed bitterly cold and turned to face the wall. I felt I had no right to be upset about your death: as a foster-child I was not allowed to grieve for you. In the morning I went to work at Boots as usual. The supervisor found me in the staff room staring at my lunchtime sandwiches, and when she heard that you had died she sent me home. She did not understand that for me there was no home. Shivering on a bench in the local park I tried to convince myself that you were dead. I tried to imagine you dead in bed but you kept opening your eyes and getting up. I considered the possibility that the Children's Department had invented lies to stop me going home. Each evening I looked in the Deaths column of the *Evening Post* but your name did not appear. When my foster-mother came out of hospital she did not mention your death. Then the Welfare Officer turned up.

'So sorry about your mum, lovey. I didn't think you would want to go to the funeral. But as you are the eldest I have brought you the few valuables found in your mum's room at the hospital.'

There was twenty pounds in cash, an old transistor radio, a cheap bracelet in a box and a pair of matching clip-on earrings. I thanked her with my frozen smile and sat clutching my inheritance.

My hopes of family reunion shattered, I felt abandoned and afraid my angry thoughts had made you die. I did not know how to face the loss of you, except to retreat into fantasy and stay stuck in denial and endless searching and raging for you and the life we could never have. I got entangled in abusive relationships with men. When I was raped I felt sure it must be my own fault and told nobody. Pregnant, I was sent to a home for unmarried mothers and had the baby adopted. I learned to hate and harm myself. I got married. Some years after your death I asked the Children's Officer why you had died. She told me you had spoken of suicide and had probably killed yourself. I got divorced. I lived alone and drank alcohol and took pills. I had long conversations with you and heard you seductively call me to join you in death. I became obsessed with finding a way for us to be united in death. There were many suicide attempts. Drug overdoses. Slashed wrists and arms. I wore your bracelet to symbolise our inextricably linked pain. I woke up in despair in intensive care units and psychiatric wards. Deep in depression, I did not understand that I was angry and mourning for you. A woman introduced me to a self-help organisation that enabled me to stop drinking and taking drugs, and this continues to be the foundation of my recovery.

Fourteen years after your death I sent for a copy of the death certificate. Cause of death is recorded as sub-arachnoid haemorrhage due to a ruptured congenital aneurism. The coroner told me there was a statement on file from a fellow staff member at the hospital, saying that you were depressed and had mentioned suicide but that the witness had not treated it seriously. I treat your anguish very grave-

ly, my mother, and I lament for you. I set out with a friend
and found your burial place. The cemetery ledger records
that no next of kin attended your funeral. Your refuge in the
earth, plot number L413, is a shared pauper's grave with no
headstone. A tree grows upon the buried bones. I placed a
bouquet of flowers against its trunk. My friend, a lay
preacher, said prayers for you and for me. I tried to cry but
still could not outwardly mourn. I felt guilty about your
lonely death and burial.

I buried myself in a second marriage. But in 1985, twenty-
two years after your death, painfully depressed, I sensed that
I needed to be alone to mourn for you. I divorced again and
went into therapy with a woman therapist. It has been a
harrowing journey, living through five years of painful and
preoccupying grief and rescuing the traumatised and abused
child within me. So much rage and despair, I thought I was
going to destroy myself. Mourning for both of us, I was so
merged with you I felt there would never be separation.
Your absence hurts. I know there is gradual transformation
in the process but the mourning is bitter and apparently life-
long. I was even ashamed of my grief for not conforming to
a textbook bereavement with a beginning, a middle and an
end. My longing to be with you does not fade, nor my deep
sorrow that you could not nurture me, that you are not here.
It is not easy to nurture myself when I am so ambivalent
about my own life.

Along the way I wrote to Social Services to find out why
we were taken into care. But the records had been
destroyed. The Children's Officer, now retired, thought she
remembered the NSPCC being involved so I contacted them
and they sent me brief notes and newspaper cuttings of the
court case. After lengthy and painful negotiations I suc-
ceeded in arranging a meeting there to obtain more information. They confirmed what I had always known but

could not fully accept into awareness. The NSPCC had intervened in our lives because you worked as a prostitute and refused to stop earning money that way. The court considered that we were in moral danger.

'DID NOT WANT HER CHILDREN'

To an attractive fur-coated blonde who told the magistrates at a west of England juvenile court that she did not want her three children, the chairman said: 'In all the years I have been sitting on the Bench I do not think I have ever made an order with greater regret.' The magistrates ordered that the children should be placed in the care of the local authority. They were before the court as being in need of care or protection. The mother, who told the court at a previous hearing that she needed twenty pounds a week to keep them, listened in silence as the chairman read a letter from a children's home describing the children as 'very pleasant and lovable children who show a great deal of affection for their mother, who has visited them regularly'. The chairman told her: 'You are asking us to take away all parental responsibility.' The mother – who admitted at a previous hearing that she had been convicted for soliciting – replied: 'The much publicised Welfare State does not provide for them. I have done my best.'

Another report adds:

The mother told the magistrates: 'Authority says I am a bad woman, and the only kind thing I can do is to let authority look after them. Whatever happens I intend to go on with my present form of life.' Chairman: 'Do you want them to know?' Mother: 'They will love me

whatever happens.' Saying that for eight years she had
had no husband, the mother went on: 'I have made lots
of sacrifices and I have paid the highest price because I
love my children and they love me. I can make a life for
myself out of nothing, because the eight years I have
toiled without a husband have taught me to do that.'
She said she had no plans for her children's future but
hoped that if they were taken into the care of the local
authority she would be able to visit them.

What was it like for you – the long years of separation? My
own pain was overwhelming for so long that I could not
contemplate yours and feel compassion – but now I do. As a
prostitute you were judged unfit to be a mother, your sexuality condemned as scandalous. In the post-war years of
affluence no one believed your plea of poverty. You did what
was unthinkable for a mother to do – you gave up your three
children and were subsequently evicted from our corpora-
tion home. You would have got little help and support from
the Children's Department to visit us and to stay in touch
regularly. They labelled you an inadequate parent and filed
you away. The Children's Officer does not recollect you nor
very much about our case. Our family was hacked to death
by the welfare state and nobody in the system remembers.

I have no photograph of you. It hurts to know so little of
your life so I wrote to the psychiatric hospital where you
died. I learned you were a waitress there in the staff restau-
rant, living in the domestic quarters. Previously you had
been a student nurse at another psychiatric hospital but you
did not complete the training as the ward work was too
much of a strain and you sought a change of direction. The
letter says you were very quiet and did not mix much with
other staff, and that this may have been a feature of your
character. The administrator could trace no one who was

friendly with you on more than a casual basis. But what choice did you really have? How could you trust anyone enough to tell them your shameful secrets? I made a pilgrimage to the hospital and was shown the old domestic quarters and the room where you lived and died. It is now a linen cupboard. The original sink was still there and I took a photograph of that. The hospital was remote and the domestic quarters far removed from the main hospital building. I got the feel of the place. It spoke of your isolation, loneliness and despair. From your bedroom window I looked towards the horizon. You died in unhope. So far I survive.

Annemie

Margaret Jacobs

There's no getting away from these big dramatic words I have to use to colour in the relationship between my mother and I. Need, ambition, anger... There's that expression, 'keeping an eye on someone'. After I'd left home for good, her eye on me was never casual. Nearly always something would give me away as shiftless, inelegant, unpurposeful: the shadows under my eyes, my haircut, thoughtless words. I was doing it wrong.

Letter, 1978

As for tensions in a marriage: Yes, there were tensions in your parents' marriage and you were aware of them and probably affected by them. But if we had known _then_ what is common knowledge _now_, about sex, about communication, about child-rearing, women's isolation in the home, without outside interest or job, without (in my case) relatives of my own and also in my case the loneliness of a migrant who was not considered a migrant (speaking the language well and 'blending into

the entourage' has distinct disadvantages!) – there
would have been that much less tension in the happy
home, I can tell you! So in case that bugs you, and is
instrumental in your rejection of men, forget it!

...What I meant at the beginning when I said this will
be the end of preaching is this: I came to a conclusion
on Saturday night. I shall detach myself from you, men-
tally and emotionally, from now on... I will still hope to
see you here, I hope you will still go out occasionally
with Dad and me; but I will not any longer think about
your life, present and future, about your emotions, your
feelings, your real 'being'. I am exactly twice as old as
you at the moment, I see your life in a much wider perspective at sixty than you can possibly do at thirty, and
what I see upsets me so much that, in fairness to
myself, to Dad and the boys, I must 'switch off' you,
other than just be in your company occasionally. To
some extent I have done that already, ever since we did
not hear from you much while overseas, but now I must
make it as total as possible. This is not blackmail, this
is for my own sake, for the protection of what is left of
my life.

The strange thing is, I have no visual memory of this typed
letter, only of the other handwritten ones. I suppose this one
hurt so much. I find it rummaging through letters from her.
As I read I feel her presence and the cut of her words. I find
myself jumping as if the words have just been written. God,
the passion! It's like a wronged lover's letter. And I can see
now things I missed then. I must have said things that
hit her where it hurt. 'Tensions in your parents' marriage
...migrant who was not considered a migrant...' I wince.

1982

I am in their bedroom. I say from a distance with a tight face, 'I want to. Do you want to talk about it?'

Mum, her voice approaching an agonised weep, says so Dad can hear, 'Charlie, she wants me to TALK about it!' (To me) 'Well, what do you want to talk about?'

She moves quickly into the kitchen, impatient to bring me to the point. I stammer, 'Well, you don't just have to... there are things people do to fight it, Arna's had cancer of all different kinds and – '

We stand in a triangle. Silence. I'm not crying. Since they told us, I've never cried with her, hugged her. She can read me: I want her to do something. Stop me being unhappy. Do something by talking. (Hadn't her doctor told me, touch her and talk to her?)

'Look,' Mum says, her face tight and body rigid. 'Look. I don't mind dying. I haven't always had a happy life.'

This shuts me up. I look at my dad. I don't know what to say. She's never said anything like this before. I haven't expected a scene like this. I don't remember what else is said, except that it feels terrible. Everyone is unhappy, I thought I'd be reaching out.

1990

Notes for my mother's portrait. I remember her concentrated straight figure waiting alone in a camel-hair coat. Gripping her bag – mouth tight with thought. Eyes alight and moving when she sees her son or daughter. She dressed neatly and with good taste, slim, stiff and apart, with a faint accent.

Doing housework, telling someone something at the

same time, fiercely. Keeping at the housework as if to stop would be dangerous. Reading at a table, head held between her hands. She never lounged. The closest she got was reading the newspaper on hands and knees on the carpet, bottom stuck out. She was different but when you grow up with difference that isn't obvious, you don't know.

We stayed at the guest house in Point Lonsdale every year when I was growing up. Mum said to me there once, 'Oh Margaret, Mrs Duncan wants me to call her Alice, I *can't...*' As if she wanted me to tell her what to do. In Hanover her family were assimilated wealthy Jews. Prussian friends called each other Frau Town Councillor X, Herr Director Y.

I never thought to myself, 'I am different.' Not that my mother and father denied that we were Jewish – it just wasn't something that was much talked about, and we had no contact with other Jews except Dad's family, and no religion. I knew that my mother had gone to school in Germany, and they had to study many more subjects than we did. In 1964 Mum wrote a memoir, about her childhood and adolescence, the school in Germany, the boarding school in England, the convent school in Belgium where she was sent to get her away from the Nazi system, her life back in Germany with her mother before they got out in 1937. To me, these were exotic tales, unconnected with the present. Our mother wasn't a migrant. She 'grew up in Germany', that was all.

1966

I am in my first year at university. In my bedroom with my mother.

'How is it with Tony?'

'All right.'

'Is he keen on you?'

'I suppose so...'

'Do you do heavy petting?'

I screw up my face, meaning yes, and it might be a problem...

'You don't really like it?'

'Oh, well, mmm...' thinking of how I don't know what to do, how to manage it, I want to kiss him and he stands there and he's kissing me and I can feel this, well, hardness against me, he's holding me close and takes his breath sort of in heaves and it's strange because he doesn't say anything about any of it...

'No. Well. I never wanted to do much of that with boys either...'

On my second day at university I'm at the swimming pool. There's no one there I know. There is a boy in a *yarmulke* who strikes up conversation as we dangle our legs in the water. For some reason I tell him I'm Jewish. I'm not very interested in him – no one I know wears a *yarmulke* – but I'm glad a male has talked to me. I tell my mother about it. She is not unsubtle, never says 'Don't get involved with that type.' She says, 'You'll never see the end of him, you won't like him, don't encourage him.' When I meet him again I see that she's right. He comes up and sticks too close. Having spoken sharply enough to discourage him, for some time I feel relieved and guilty when I see him.

I never lost the instinct to confide in my mother.

1981

Foggy, generalised memories; walking, elaborate food preparations, beach. I've been in a relationship with Helen for a couple of years. We're on holiday at Mallacoota. I remember wanting us to lie on a bed looking out over the inlet to the mountains. Thinking that if this happens it will be a happy thing. It happens, but isn't quite what it is supposed to be.

Except for the day I rang Mum and Dad. Must've been a good day, I'm jaunty and have remembered I should do the right thing and phone them. On the way to the phone we see King Parrots in the street and watch them for a while. In the booth I dial the number and there's no answer. I feel unreasonably panicky. Where are they? Relief, I've forgotten the area code. Dad answers. My voice high and cheery says hullo. Dad's voice is flat and uninterested. They'd been away, but Mum hadn't been well. That's not unusual. But Dad's usually pleased to hear from me. I hang up with a feeling of resentfulness that doesn't quite get shaken off.

The announcements. A month or so later? Made separately to each of their children. Mum has refused to see Helen but rings her at work and tells her. Would she make sure she is with me on such and such a night when they are going to tell me? So I won't have to spend the night alone? Evening. They stand on the doorstep. 'We've got some bad news.' They see from my face I think one of my brothers has died in an accident. No one has been killed. They tell me in the hall. She's got stomach cancer. She's not expected to live more than two years. Three may be possible – they can't predict. Mum and Dad tell me about her doctor. He's very good. Not putting pressure on her to have an operation. It's quite advanced. Huge operation. Risk. She doesn't want it. She doesn't want fuss, she wants everything to go on the same for as long as possible.

It's happened. I'm frightened – she's going to die and I

haven't done anything. Ulcerative colitis, very bad for years.
What I always feared. I've always said to myself, you must
talk to her. Get her to see someone. She'd touch her stomach every so often and sort of stiffen and recoil. I didn't dare
say, 'I think there's something wrong.'

That confidence I couldn't manage. Our confidences had
never been about her, they'd been about me. The one about
Helen, not long before. I'm trying to appease her anger and
fear about what I say I am. Her fear that I won't have kids.

'But Mum, I AM happy! It's lovely with Helen, and the
kids.'

'Can't you see, you're the sucker? You might think you're
happy now, you enjoy the kids, but you'll break up
eventually, she'll go off with the kids and you'll be left with
nothing!'

(I can't stop myself telling Helen what she's said. Then I
feel that my mother is still running the show – she's got to
me – I despise myself...) She's angry, I think she's sick,
there's something wrong, I should talk to her. I don't.

Some months after they'd told us about mum, I talked to
the naturopath. Wasn't there anything you could do with
stomach cancer, apart from the orthodox treatments? She
said a grapes-only diet had been suggested by a doctor. I
couldn't face that Mum wouldn't want to try these treatments. Fear of the future paralysed me in the present. About
Mum that is; I could do other things. Things I had put off. I
bought a car, went to Italian summer school, landed a full-
time job that wasn't teaching. Mum was pleased about the
job. Replaced the glass in the front window. Helen and I
spent some balmy days at the beach: I wasn't unhappy.

Italian summer school threw up a hurdle of fear though. Helen's friend Arna would be at the entrance and I might have to talk to her; she'd been fighting cancer in different forms for years and refusing all orthodox treatment, with success. I didn't ask myself why I was so petrified of seeing her...

1982

Mum decided she'd make me curtains for my house. We got the tram into town to find material. Rummaging through bolts of material – I knew what Mum liked and it wasn't what I really wanted – but I'm not good at choosing curtain material. I picked out a dark green hessian for my bedroom. She liked a delicately patterned half-shiny material for the living room, and I said to myself, yes, I can cope with that, she thinks it's right... Coles cafeteria then for a cup of tea and something to eat. She was so thin, I wished she'd eat more. But it was good to be on this kind of outing with my mother.

We got on the tram. The conductor was someone I knew and I introduced her to Mum. We changed trams. Mum sniffed and pursed her lips.

'What's the matter?'

'Oh, you ask me why. Why do all your friends have that look – that lesbian look? So unattractive. It upsets me – oh, I don't know...'

I didn't know where to start – I'd forgotten that my mother hadn't stopped feeling all those things. I'd been glad she'd seen one of my friends who'd shown such warmth. 'She's a lovely woman!' I said weakly. The good mood of our day was gone.

I visited Mum in hospital, took her a tiny posy of flowers from my garden. They brought her a tray with four bowls of jelly, each a different colour. Each bowl was a different kind of food. Was it another visit or that one when Mum gave me her gold signet ring?

'I can't wear it anymore – I'm too thin. I want you to have it – do you want it?'

This was the ring Uncle Eric wore and then she wore it after his death. It used to be their father's, one of them had always worn it.

'I asked John if he wanted it but he didn't.'

So something had been passed to me: I wore it.

Called to the hospital one morning soon after. They said she'd had a bad night and wouldn't live long. Mum was still in the shared ward. She introduced me to the woman in the next bed who'd had a stroke. Mum whispered that she felt sorry for her.

'That's what my mother was like, it's the most awful thing.'

Mum was to be moved. We waited in the corridor, and then went into her little room.

'I asked them why I'm being put here. They said to give me privacy. I don't think that's why. They don't want me to be seen. I would upset people.'

I phoned Mum's two friends. Waited in the corridor. Dad came out and said he and Mum had had a talk and she'd said goodbye. Dad and my brothers and I ate white bread sandwiches out of a machine downstairs. When we went back in Mum asked what day it was. Dad said,

'It's the 27th May; tomorrow is your birthday.'

'Birthday, deathday!' said Mum.

We said to each other in the corridor: 'She goes in and out.' At night we came back from having something to eat. She would sleep, then call out. It went on too long. She wasn't neat any more. We made helpless, ineffectual gestures towards her. She was tossing and moaning and throwing the covers off. We asked the nurses for the injection. They couldn't because it wasn't four hours; they were kids. We were indignant but did nothing. She moaned, 'Let me go.'

After the injection they left us alone with her. It was past midnight, her birthday. She was slowing down. She stopped, died. It seemed there was nothing the matter.

1982

June. Arna wrote to me about my mum dying. Something about how she'd heard I hadn't said what I wanted to my mother before her death. That I should say it anyway. I had a terrible feeling of omission on reading this. But it was presumptuous, what she was saying...I pushed it away.

Taking Mum's clothes in armfuls into the Brotherhood shop. But she'd worked for the Brotherhood! I looked at the women taking the clothes from me, such clean clothes in such good repair and felt like saying that they were from my mother who's died. Felt that to say this would be cruel. Then something about their closed faces told me that they recognised the situation anyway.

It had happened. You had to 'get on with life'. She was dead. It wasn't the end of everything. I didn't think about her very much. I worried about my father and my job.

1984

Jen held my hand and helped me to look out the window on a flight back from Adelaide. I didn't have to be terrified of flying then! I'd always dreamed about Europe but been too afraid to fly so far. Perhaps after what had happened I could face life as a gamble...

1985

Overseas. As I had been led to expect, so it was. The highs very high and the lows dramatically, galvanizingly low. No grey fuzzy patches of memory from that time. I wrote to myself: 'Oh Paris. Swish down streets in the rain. The markets opening, closing, opening – 'Vendredi, tout est fini... Australienne? Kangourou!' The African man selling me the pimentos in Rue Mouffetard – laughing at me. Suddenly seeing the sweep of buildings uphill and downhill in Avenue Claude Bernard – its blueness against the slate sky. Leaving for England, I wrote: 'No more speaking French. Those small conversations – you measure your words, leave spaces between sentences; relish and register the person behind the eyes. I'm different in French.'

1986

Just the same in Australia though. The anti-climax of being home in Melbourne. No proper job. From time to time I'd feel moved to tell the story of my visit to the Maison St Pierre convent in Ghent. 'The most amazing experience', I'd say and explain how I'd been shown into the same ante-room my mother had entered as a boarder. I felt I never did justice to the story, which always ended with: 'I couldn't stop myself from crying.' Hoping that my listener would show me where to go from there. No one did.

Things with my friends were bad. Helen was in a new relationship. I'd made a fool of myself over Louis. I was anxious, possessive, super-vulnerable, a victim. It didn't take much prompting for me to agree I should 'see someone'. I'd never committed myself to seeing a counsellor before – being 'in therapy' was a term avoided in my circle at that time.

Sitting in the car outside the counsellor's house I'd have to draw breath before facing her. Dragging it all out: what happened with Lou. Anger, guilt and fear with that. And Mum. Miriam was the person to tell me about it: the daughter of German Jews who'd been in camps, she knew the story. She might have put herself down, but no one was good enough for your mother, she said. Upper class with a whole culture of music, books and servants and then in Australia in the forties, what was there for her?

'Yes,' I said, 'I suppose she was – '

I stopped. A snob. What else could I find out, if I could dare to think this?

1988 Axe dream

My mother is having a go at chopping wood.
Her handbag is slipping down from her shoulder
over her arm her chopping arm
I go to tell her this is happening
She doesn't listen

Early 1990

Until this year Mum's memoir with the photo of her on the top that Dad put on has sat in the bookcase, unread for years. It needs editing, I'd always said, embarrassed by what I thought were naïvely expressed politics on the rise of

Hitler, and its bits of flowery English. I'd avoid letting my eyes fall on it, even.

If people asked about my mother I'd say that in a way I was relieved. Since she'd died I'd made a lot of changes, things had got better for me. I'd tell them how glad I was that I'd been there when she died, that it had helped me to acknowledge that she was gone. How I'd worn her ring continuously since she gave it to me; that I felt something positive came from her to me through the gift of the ring. (Even though, as I told people, it turned out she hadn't offered it to John at all. Why had she said she had? In order to be able to give it to me?) I kept reciting these stories and the one about the visit to the Maison St Pierre convent when I'd cried. They'd become a sort of 'memory of Mum' rosary – a way of not looking.

No one can make you remember.

Visiting the Maison St Pierre

I'm standing in the front parlour in the Maison St Pierre showing a photograph to a nun. She's looking at me searchingly but not unsympathetically. I tell her in French that my mother has died since this photo was taken in 1973. Here. Mum and Mother Selina. It's a plea for her to understand me, who I am. I don't explain, Annemarie Meyer, German, Jewish, boarder pupil here in the thirties – just stupidly show the photo. I'm surprised and embarrassed by little sobs forming with the words and tears forming as I am asking her: is this nun in the photo with my mother still here? Can I see her? What was the phrase she used in reply, the equivalent of 'passed away' in French?

'I'm sorry, Mother Selina is no longer with us...?'

The furniture in the room is old and formal and elegant. I stumble over the words:

'It's the same room as in the 1930s?' – feeling ridiculous.

Of course it is. I'm thinking about the scene in my mother's book where she and her mother are received into a little parlour at the front of the convent, in 1934.

'I'm afraid this is not a good time for us, many of us have influenza – or it would be possible for you to be shown around the convent – if you had telephoned us you could have come at a better time. It's a pity!'

It had never occurred to me to ring, I don't think I could have. I explain that I'm staying in Brussels – this is my only day in Ghent. I'm still trying to get the better of my little sobs.

'You've come from Australia? Are you married?'

'No, I'm not.' My voice is still choked.

'If you would like to come into the other room – would you take some coffee?'

There's a kind of distant pity in her bearing; she won't let me leave in tears.

I'm left sitting in the other front room across the hall. Sniffling. It's a big building. The nun comes back with strong coffee and a plate with two large and expensive elegant cakes. They go down with that lumpy salty taste food has if eaten when you are upset. She doesn't have anything to eat or drink. Of course, they don't eat with the non-religious. She keeps me busy with talk.

She's going to show me just a little of the convent before I have to go. We go past a glassed-off section in the hall. There's a woman sitting inside it. Some explanation of my presence goes on. I'm still clutching my photo, which I show her. She's quite effusive towards me.

'Ah – I remember – yes, that one who was – (some word I

didn't understand).'

I'm confused. Does she really remember my mother? She doesn't seem to react to the 1973 photo. I can't begin to describe my mother at sixteen. My host nun has already continued up the corridor.

'Elle est polonaise,' she says – as if to cast some doubt on the authority of a Pole.

She gestures out into the courtyard. I try to imagine it without the ugly additions but can't. A door opens and then shuts but in time for me to see a teenage boy. In this convent! In my mum's day the nuns never went outside the convent and the only man allowed inside was the priest.

'Oh yes, everything is changed. Flemish is spoken now in the convent, not French.'

As she's showing me another corridor I tell her I have a message from my father. Did the convent receive the copy of the chapter from my mother's memoir about the Maison St Pierre which he sent them after his visit here in 1983?

'Oh, there are many books in the archives...'

The tour has finished. We re-enter the hall.

'If you telephone us from Brussels, you will be very welcome to come back when there is not so much influenza. Then you will be able to be shown around...'

1985

February 2nd. 'Legacy of Horror', feature article from *The Age* newspaper:

In the late seventies in America an organisation called Second Generation was formed to help the children of survivors, then aged between about twenty and thirty-five, who had never been able to talk about their problems...

Recognising some of my family's traits in these accounts I had cut out the article and filed it.

Had Mum been a Holocaust survivor? She hadn't been in a camp...

Mid-1990

Started taking Mum's memoir away on holidays with me: I'd known for a while I had to read it. But I couldn't open it. Then I did, and there was Europe in the twenties and thirties: streets, houses, relatives. I'd go back into it nearly every night, savouring it. But after the first few chapters it became a story. My mum's story. Might have been a different book altogether from the one I remembered. Before, I'd always skipped through it to the bit where you'd get a quick thrill of horror: Mum's mother is summoned by the Gestapo. Mum waits alone in the flat in Hanover until she comes back.

But the book is about a girl gradually losing her world, told without melodrama or self-pity. Her best friend, Gichen, who said,

'But Annemie, Hitler doesn't mean Jews like you!'

The attraction between the two of them is implicit. At the convent, the beautiful Mother Marie Claire; Mum and she had corresponded till the sixties. Gichen and the nun, I realised, were the two most powerfully and passionately recreated characters in the story. 'What,' I thought to myself, 'is the Meaning of This?'

As I read, the mother I'd known became a person who'd existed before me, as a child, a young wife. The two images of my mother, the one I'd known and the unreal 'childhood in Germany' one, coalesced.

1990

I have read nearly to the end of the story. A letter arrives suggesting I write for an anthology of pieces by women whose mothers have died. I make notes. I cry a bit, writing about Mum and her hot-water bottle. The comfort she got from it. I look back at the notebook after a few days. Most of it's about the hot-water bottle and the rest seems too morbid.

I'm reading *SYBIL: The true story of a woman possessed by sixteen separate personalities*. I enter a quote in my notebook: 'Memories make a person mature emotionally.' What am I forgetting?

Late 1990

I write. I can't write. I try to go back; I tell stories, make notes, reread Mum's memoir. One day I find myself wedged into an armchair seething. I am confronting her doctor: Why weren't you there? The shit way you let people die, only young nurses there and no morphine when she needed it and why didn't you warn us at least?

There it comes, that sensation I get. When I drive past the hospital... someone says something about pain... a fluttery sensation of something not as obvious as guilt, just shaken off, skipped over. I'm reminded of the night I went round unexpectedly and she was in pain, needing me to get the tablets. I remember only so far, the shock of her helplessness – and stop. There are conversations I should have, properly, past times I should mull over, with my brothers, my father, someone, but I don't.

I write: 'The skin on my neck crawls as I ask myself – how could she eat? How did she feel? Did she really want to die?'

Then I think: Why didn't *I* ask? Why wasn't *I* there? I wince, turn my head. To think that she needed something from me, that only I could give. I think that might have been so.

But now, ten years later, have I still got time to cry? Still got time to face remembering? My memories – so often passed over, diluted by fear; my anger too damp to ignite. You have to keep looking for things the anger and fear might belong to. To do this, do you have to be by yourself, for minutes, hours, days, years? I don't know. Perhaps it's not so much *looking* for things as watching. I dream my mother is one of several people lying suspended in hammock beds. Hanging there insistently talking to me: she wants me to keep what she is telling me secret. I wake and remember the dream and think, 'Why don't I feel bad?' She never could ask me that while she was alive. But the image of her there is so strong.

You have to go on watching, asking the questions, finding the stories.

Mother

Marilyn Hacker

I was born when she was thirty-eight.
Pleated secrets sunlit on a skirt
spread over rocks, dark curls, sharp nose, alert
shopgirl's cautious mouth-curve. She had to wait
between high school and college, married late
 – thirty-one – motherless, teen-aged, serving
father, time black-frocked at Macy's, deserving
Jewish daughter. Patience: her great
longings encysted with it, burst. I'll be
thirty-eight in November. In her head
whir words she learned, memorized, accented
impeccably out of the Bronx. In the Bronx she
rages, shrunken, pillow-propped, in a rank
room. I invent freedom at the bank.

I invent stories she will never tell.
I was fatherless; she was motherless.
I thought that I was motherless as well.
Harridan, pin-curled in a washed-out housedress,
she scrubbed the tiny kitchen on all fours

and sniped. I bolted. I told dog-walkers,
as I chipped bark flakes from the sycamore
out front, such stories! I do not know hers.
The mother says, 'When I was twenty, I...'
The daughter, 'I was... I never thought to tell you...'
'My best friend was...' 'I was afraid. Tell me why...?'
'... I was afraid.' Twined down the long wind go
fictions, afternoon lies the nurse tells to
a furious old woman, who will die.

The Distance Between Them

Sally St Clair

At the funeral, the vicar, whom I didn't know at all, said she was a saint. He said she was a wonderful mother and a wonderful wife who had always had time to help other people. He said she would be missed by many people. Well, I miss her. I miss her because she was my mother. Apart from that, there is nothing for me to miss: I never knew who she was, and so what I will always miss – forever – is the chance to find out. And I think that she died to make sure she didn't ever have to find out.

She was the daughter her middle-aged mother had longed for. A sweet little curly-haired sister for my Uncle Stuart, her grown-up brother. Probably she was a shock to my grandfather, at least he always looked shocked to me. Later she became the second wife of a father of two children whose mother had died. Then there were all of us. And of course she was also a teacher. But what she wanted and liked and hated, and what made her laugh and what made her sad, I just don't know. The thing is that I doubt whether she ever did herself. It was part of her religion – we were Exclusive Brethren – if she felt a feeling coming on, any feeling at all really, she crushed it down. She would not acknowledge it, so all those feelings had to go somewhere and they all bunched up together and began to eat into her. She had cancer, my mother. They chopped it out from one bit, but, in the end, it escaped and just crept around my mother's body till it found a place where it was safe.

The day before she died, my sister and I made her bed and she said she wanted yellow sheets and we looked at each other in amazement across her lying there. She must have thought we were irritated and quickly said it wasn't important. Oh no, we said, it's terribly important. Then we could not get those yellow sheets quickly enough and we laid them over and under her poor old body. And that was the only thing I ever heard my mother say she wanted.

She was a very perfect mother. We had Chilprufe vests, and a rocking horse, and a playroom with French windows, and a big house with an old orchard where we played, and she spent her evenings smocking and sewing and darning. In the mornings she was always up first and into the huge cold bathroom to wash and dress. She bought cheap and serviceable material and sewed dresses for herself in an hour, every one the same pattern. When she died, my father was annoyed that she'd gone without tidying up and asked me to take her clothes. So I took twenty-nine identical dresses from her wardrobe and folded them into dustbin bags and brought them to my house and put them in the attic. My sister told me that my mother had said once that she'd always thought herself ugly and so what was the need of dressing up? But my mother was beautiful. When I was very little she had long hair, black curls, to her waist. She would brush it and then wind it up around a velvet band, like all the Brethren women. I wonder if they all brushed their hair while they looked into a small high mirror so they could not see it. But I saw it. She cut it all off when I was seven and we left the Brethren. My father had begun to disagree with the doctrine. Perhaps she was fed up with plaiting four heads of hair each morning as we ate the cooked breakfasts she had prepared. We never had just cereal and milk. Sometimes I stayed the night with a friend who had a less than perfect mother and we would eat cornflakes in the morning. My stomach, used to substantial amounts of bacon and egg first thing, would complain and grumble all through lessons and I would long for a break and an iced bun.

My mother was huge and always on a diet. She made us meat pie but she ate cottage cheese and boiled cabbage. We had cold ham and soldiers of bread with boiled eggs and she had a hard-boiled egg (to stay longer in her stomach) and two Energen rolls. Once she let me make supper and I made lasagne which I'd had at my friend's house (her parents were artists; I thought they were exciting and my parents thought they were corrupting me) but my father would not eat it. He said it was foreign and my mother made him a cold meat salad with piccalilli. The others liked the lasagne and I think my mother did too, but she did not want to betray my father. We never had lasagne again. Now my mother is dead, my father makes curry out of the Aga cookbook. I suppose that isn't really foreign at all.

After breakfast we went to school. We all wore school uniforms and my mother washed and ironed eight pink dresses each week and all the white shirts my brothers wore. There were two of them and four of us and my mother held three on each hand and crossed us over the main road and we went to school. We were set apart from the rest because we lived by the main entrance where teachers drove through and so we did not go into school by the children's entrance. I expect my father arranged that. We were also set apart because our mother was so perfect that, although there were six of us, we always had the correct uniform. Once, in assembly, the Headmistress asked us all to come to the front. One in every class we were, except class three. My mother had had a miscarriage. The Headmistress showed us to the rest of the school, those whose mothers were not so perfect and those who came to school untidy or not correctly dressed or even dirty. And I had to lift the hem of my skirt and show the whole school that even my knickers were absolutely perfect. I hated them all after that. But I knew my mother was the best in the world.

Every summer holiday, my parents rented a house by the seaside and we played on the beach and swam and made new friends and my father discussed doctrine with the local men who'd left the Brethren and my mother sat knitting in a deckchair on the promenade or in the beach hut. She would gaze out across the sand to where we were, and as far as she was concerned, it was just like home. Except that we had two breakfasts; the first one of cold milk and cereal, early, before the Seaside Mission Bible Study. The second, a nice, warming cooked breakfast. Then we went to the beach service and she did housework and shopping and packed a picnic lunch to take to the beach hut.

In the next beach hut to us was a family of three children and they had a nice nanny who wore a uniform and sometimes took her belt off to walk on the sand. Occasionally the mother of the children came too, but she wasn't a proper mother at all. She had a special sunbed on which she lay far down the beach away from her children. I would watch her for hours, fascinated, as she lay motionless in the sun, her eyes closed and her thin golden body glistening with oil. When her children cried, she remained still, and when their nurse made tea, she would get changed and drive away. There were no other mothers like that that I knew. She seemed to have another life, but it was not one that I could imagine. I wondered what she did, and where she went to, alone, without her children. She was unreal to me.

Each May my mother's birthday came again. She preferred to forget it, but we, with childish enthusiasm, wanted otherwise. We wanted her to stay in bed while we made her a fine breakfast, but she never would, and so that special day began just like any other day and she got up first. One year my father bought her steak for her dinner while we ate pork chops. She struggled to eat the thick and bloody slab of meat, her face red with weeping, while we watched in embarrassment, bewildered by her reaction and fearful of the growing anger of our father. We were the distance between them; as we grew up and left home in the same order that we had come into it, the distance narrowed and there was nothing left to absorb the pain between them, and so my mother and my father built a new barrier of silence.

For her birthday one year I made a grey silk handkerchief case embroidered with lilies of the valley because she once told me she liked them. I spent my pocket money on a tiny square bottle of perfume in the big department store in our town. Years later, rummaging in her bureau, I found the case, carefully folded, and the little bottle of perfume, unopened and the label faded. My mother never wore scent, though my father would have liked her to. He wanted her to wear silk blouses, but she never would, and he fretted in his desire to buy them for her.

We watched him grow bitter with longing to touch her and we saw her stiffen as he passed. She wore a corset which held her up and inwards and her great body felt hard and unyielding to our childish hands. I would wonder that she could ever sit or bend. When I was eight, I told my friends at school that she was my nurse and imagined that my real mother was a tall slender woman with sparkling eyes and a body that swayed like a thin tree in the wind.

When she died my father let us sit around her body. Before she grew cold, so we could think she was only asleep, we stroked her hands and breasts and wound her hair in our fingers. Her hands were so small and fragile; when I lifted them, they lay in mine like those of a little child. Sitting there together, we realised that we had not known for a very long time the feel of her, the softness of her skin and hair. I think we had not known that since we were babies: then we must have touched her, though I don't remember. But I do remember this – my mother, drowsing in an armchair on a hot afternoon, with the youngest asleep on her lap, their bodies folded together, heavy and still, her hands cradling the baby.

For all my childhood, I watched her hands. I could not bear the emptiness of her eyes, so I watched her hands ironing and sewing, chopping and stirring and knitting. Always knitting. She sat and knitted, her hands flashing in front of her, while her eyes watched television. I could not take my eyes away from her hands. Once, a long time ago, when I was pregnant, I began to knit as she had taught me. Two rows of fine white wool, then I laid it down. I did not want to be that kind of mother. So instead I dreamt the months away and in my dreams I became the perfect mother, the one I never had.

And my daughter always had the best I could get. I bought her nappies in Harrods and she wore handmade shoes. She grew up beautiful and healthy with the food I gave her every day and I told her all the things I knew I should. But my daughter never touches me except when she comes home from boarding school and we hug each other because I am her mother and she is my daughter and so we should. But we never get any closer. I suppose I just don't know how to do it, I never learnt.

Silhouette on the Wall

Rahila Gupta

Symbols of continuity – a kaftan I sleep in, stitched by her – link me to the shadow on the wall. Done in charcoal from a photo of her silhouette taken by some pompous admirer of hers who rather fancied his artistry. Very useful, though, in the search for something to immortalise her in my very mortal memory. There was plenty to ritualise and ease the pain of her passing when it happened. Relatives swept aside our freethinking, at a point of emotional weakness, with a series of archaic Hindu rituals. Now, year after year on the anniversary, there seems no adequate ritual for unbelievers. For twelve years, my father placed an advert in *The Times of India* – her photo with words of grieving.

I used to light an eternal candle – something about a light flickering to stay alive against an ever-depleting wax base comforted me. But it felt artificial (I had borrowed it from the Jewish tradition). So I dumped it one year, and now I range from giving up smoking for the day to sending a cheque to a cancer research organisation.

Artificial – this need to mourn her death, once a year, when I remember her daily in my living, replicating her recipes, sulking in my relationships, sitting on my pride and refusing to budge, feeling her lack of confidence erode my actions. Her deep sensitivity that makes my eyes sting when someone ventures a criticism. Her need to be validated, her ability to appear strong when everything was crumbling inside her. Her ridiculous levels of honesty coursing through my veins. So what's new? My indulgence of my children rebelling against the regime she forced me into. My inability to sew – whether I break with her traditions or continue them, she laid down the baseline. But that baseline is already thirteen years old. That is my grieving: that we cannot grow together, that we can no longer interact, that my memory of her is fixed in time and at a particular point of my own development. That is why there is comfort in doing something she had known me to do or wearing something she had seen me in.

The memory of her last months, eaten away by cancer, has a way of wiping away the time I spent with her. The experience I most wanted to share with her – motherhood – came after her death. What we shared was that neither of us had a lap to lay our heads in when mothering began to drain our energies. Her mother had died when she was only twelve. Reading my diaries to fill out the patchwork memories I have of her, I found only petty quarrels and jealousies. No siblings with whom to refine and deepen my recollections. This patchwork I offer myself and my children.

Remember how I thought she must be my stepmother because she was so strict with me. Remember hunting for pictures of her with me as a baby – just to make sure I wasn't adopted – and when she told me that in the earliest picture I was only two months old, I started asking questions about the earliest age at which a baby could be adopted.

Remember how she would chase me round the dining table when my father went abroad on business so that she could catch me and beat me. And how her sister would come for me from the other end when my agility became too much for my mother. Remember how they would cook their awful Gujarati food when my father was away and allow me to wither away from starvation.

Remember the time she beat me on my back with a broom handle when I was only four and my father bought me an ice-cream – risked her wrath to show me his love. And I was only pretending that the ash in the ashtray was my snuffbox and was faking a sneeze after I had snuffled it in.

Remember the time a journalist friend of my father had come to stay and brought a cardboard box of heavy tomes to help him write his history of how all world languages were born from Punjabi and we discovered a massive pile of *Playboys* at the bottom. My mother and I looked through them – she sharing all my naïvety and shock, talking about sex and male genitalia with wide-eyed wonder as though she shared my lack of experience.

Remember the time my father slipped and fractured his wrist because he had had one too many whiskies – she didn't talk to him for six weeks (all the time the plaster was on) and my father had to ask my aunt to part his hair in the middle.

Remember the time a business associate had presented us with a large basket of fruit during Diwali and my mother refused to touch them because she thought he was trying to bribe my father.

Remember how she cried as she looked at the old curtains refashioned from my thick green school uniform, saying, 'Your father never invests money in this house.' Shocked by the strength of her feelings. Reinforcing my feeling that she would have lived longer if she had let her attention be engaged by something outside the house. That tailoring shop that she loved yet would only get to by 2 p.m. when the attendant opened it at 9 a.m. Because she couldn't

finish all her housework. All that talent and London return
diploma in cutting which put her a cut above the others.
Spending hours taking a collar out of *Vogue*, a sleeve style
out of *Bouda* and putting together a dress for me, exacting
her price – hours of tweezing her grey hair out because she
was too proud to have it dyed. And when the end came I
wasn't even there.

Living in England, news from home gets distorted by distance and time and expectations. What started as a pimple
on my mother's face gradually became a cancerous sore –
not in time or by medical default but by the staggered way
in which the news was filtered through to me. An aunt
invited me to dinner to give me the news. 'They didn't want
to write to you,' she said, 'in case you fainted from shock' –
a logic which immediately raised my suspicions. I didn't
understand why I should be shocked by a pimple on which
they were going to operate. The word 'operation', however,
had its sobering effect – but why a pimple, why this interest
in plastic surgery at this time of life? I was asked to visit, to
return seven thousand miles, to borrow money for my fare
– and I thought, 'No, it's a pimple, I'll stay till after the summer sales and pay my fare with my overtime earnings.'

Not being able to penetrate my unfrightened state, relatives could not persuade me to go. So they resurrected the
truth in one short cruel statement. Took the next flight out.
A request for liquid food. She wrote and asked for powdered,
easy-to-make soups. I took 175 packets in my enthusiasm to
please – at one a day, they outlived her by four. Bulk quantities of every minor request as if she would be obliged to
live until she finished each item. My mother hated waste.

I risked the wrath of the Bombay customs. Each Knorr
packet tucked between books and knickers. Customs saw
the books, saw the passport. Thought, 'Student!' Thought,
'British!' Chewed paan but wouldn't put the clearance chalk

marks on my suitcase. I looked through the smoked-up glass twenty yards away and saw a hand above the sea of heads – long, tapering fingers reduced to bones, consumed by the lengthening shadow of disease but still the hand that had stung my adolescent cheek. My eyes poked into that rattling, skeletal hand, searching for clues of what the face might have become, afraid to confront the evidence directly. Will she have time to recognise what I have become? Looked at the customs man, saw perversity and thought, 'Bastard! My mother is dying.' And all the time the restless skeleton caught my eye.

I had come home, she had to go abroad. Hospital after specialist hospital. No, we can't treat you. Go home. Just like that. Not even a word of comfort to raise hopes crushed and money humiliatingly borrowed, so ill-spent. And all because an Indian doctor said, unguardedly, 'In America there is this new drug, platinum.'

Found a hospital which would cater for her dying needs. The alarm was set for seven, but at a quarter to six I was fumbling for the light switch, dispelling dreams of a clear-skinned face, the scars gone, the pus-filled wounds dry – only the shadow of what was fell across her face. Half-asleep, stumbled to the phone to check on arrival time. Walked to the corner to buy some cigarettes. Ambulance arrived on time, trusted man ready to leave me behind. I fight with him, 'You could've picked me up at the corner.' 'The ambulance is not a taxi,' he mutters.

Trip back to the hospital in a jolting ambulance – a painful anticipation of potholes. Trying to keep her from sliding off the stretcher, dividing attention unequally so as not to notice her decline. Catching her breath, she says, 'I nearly died last night.' If not for an emergency injection, my father tells me later. It is that 'nearly' that is peculiar to her condition, an inch closer always but never at the end.

Hospital: endless corridors, trolley careering madly down in chase of the elusive doctor on duty. Admit her, admit her, please. An endless wait, hunger and inefficiency. Peon waiting mealy-mouthed for baksheesh.

Finally, a cold white room, peeling the sticky nylon sari from her bones and removing shoes hanging limply on her feet. Finally, the most pressing problem over. Pessaries, long-awaited catharsis, purgation ripping her bowels clean. What a long night, punctuated by cigarette burns and forty winks. Consoling myself with truisms, time flies. After every hour, a minute passes. She is not even troublesome enough to help me pass the time. Reading *The Sound and the Fury*, letting words flow over me, meaningless music jarring my tired senses. Give her sleep, she needs it. I must fight it.

It took another twenty-two days. Moved her within five days to a nursing home where doctors from any brand of medicine could practise and we wouldn't have to smuggle the homoeopath in as a fake relative. And when we left the nursing home it was the only time in her illness when a crowd of auxiliaries didn't gather for the obligatory tip, because we were leaving for the crematorium.

The hospital where she was treated before she left for America in search of a cure – the best in town, specialist cancer hospital, a charitable institution, run by Tatas, industrial benefactors in the manner of Joseph Rowntree. Coming from England, shocked at my father's complacency. Is this the best? The peon would not bring my mother's file in time to see the doctor if she did not bribe him with a rupee. When the doctor arrived a crowd of patients ran after him from treatment room to treatment room, like groupies after a pop star. My mother too would be part of that horde whilst I would attack from another angle, whoever got in first. But that was while she still had her strength. Then you would see the same people three months later sitting on the bench unable to run anymore, debilitated, while their husbands, daughters and brothers ran on their behalf. And when they reached the doctor, they would shout across to the patient who would squeeze through the crowd.

Even to get there, I would have to fold my mother's increasingly limp body into the crowded bus and stand jam-packed tight behind her to stop her crumpling into a heap. Only an hysterical outburst with my father won me the right to take her by taxi. Of course, it was a luxury especially when my father was temporarily unemployed. Walking up the drive of the hospital – pots, pans and shredded mattresses rolled up, people crouching by them, relatives of patients from the rural areas who could not afford even the most run-down guest houses. Crowds of patients squatting in the hospital corridors, a child with the most massive lumps bulging out of his neck and shoulders, a woman sitting with a handkerchief covering her mouth and when the handkerchief slipped temporarily, she had no chin.

Foreign doctors from the Sloane-Kettering Institute in New York and Royal Marsden in London tailing the Indian doctors – exchange programmes giving them exposure to the widest range of cancers in the shortest periods of time.

Yes, the hospital was good. I had already been in Bombay too long. Had got used to different standards. Seen the other public hospitals, seen the bloodied sheets of mattresses lying between beds, underneath beds, in aisles and corridors and compared the standards with Tata Cancer Hospital. Remember the race for my mother's WBC (White Blood Corpuscles) count. She could not have her twice-weekly jab of chemotherapy if her WBC count was low. And when she missed even one jab, the lumps would come marauding over her face, some splitting open into a seething white and red mass, emitting the smell of death. Even the skin that was left – a thinned grey membrane with cigarette holes in it where the lumps had erupted. Miles I would walk in the blazing sun, looking for good quality fruit and vegetables, to find the ingredients for my latest recipe, colourful and aesthetically presented to hide the bland boring taste for a palate used to spices but so sensitised by medicine that even salt burned. I would count the number of mouthfuls of protein – because protein was the secret ingredient of the WBC count. And when we got to the hospital, I would wait with bated breath while we were told, yes, she could have a jab. Yes, I was thrilled for her to have yet another jab of cancer-threatening but also life-threatening medication.

What a struggle to get her to eat. How I fought with her on days when my hopes for her lay low – how could she be so selfish, if she wouldn't co-operate in saving her life, how could I do it alone? And then the last day before the naso-gastric tube was fitted, I had burst into tears that would never stop because she had refused her food, and an uncle visited and, looking at my tears, feared the worst – but no, it was just that she refused to eat. And the sheer pleasure of unopposed and completely undisciplined pouring in of pints of the most nutritious fluids – milk, chicken soup, grape juice (acting on the dictates of a book called *The Grape Cure of Cancer*) sobering only when her body rebelled with uncontrolled diarrhoea.

And I would watch her when she lay asleep, imagining this is how she would look, trying to feel the grief in stages like payments on credit so that the final flood would not deluge me. Only three days before she died did she become delirious. My friend who had spent the last seventeen days with me on the twenty-two hour day shift – my father relieved me for two hours every day so that I could go home for a shower, a meal and a stiff whisky – thought it a joke when my mother accused an uncle of pinching the soap which my friend was looking for to wash her hands. I knew then that the end was near, but hope is so disconcertingly irrepressible. Even the night before she died, there was a distinguished crowd of urinologists advising us on the urine cure of cancer. I could have sworn that the homoeopathic injections in the neck had begun to dry her wounds. Only the rest of her couldn't wait.

And the sheer drama of reality. The day her body gave up was the first day my friend went home to see her father and make sure he was OK. He was lying unconscious in a pool of vomit. And partly to escape the rituals of an Indian funeral in which people besiege your home every day and unknown family beat their chests, grab you and sob as if their world was giving out while you stand there feeling hard as nails, I stayed with my friend while she watched over her father in hospital. Coming home only very late in the evening, my heart would sink as I saw a row of sandals and shoes ranged by the front door. Only when the crowds stopped coming did the loss begin to sink in.

The day her body gave up, or was it her will, I had gone home unexpectedly at lunchtime because by now all my aunts and uncles had come to stay and help. The relief of the change in routine gave a sharp edge to my hunger for lunch. But before lunch I was called back to the hospital. Funny how the sun is always shining on days when your world is crumbling. A crowd of medicos around my mother's bed and I can only watch through the open door because my feet will take me no further. The bed is reclined in the opposite direction, her feet at an angle above her head and her body convulses obscenely while a man pumps up and down over her breast. My mouth opens like the horse from *Guernica* and I sink to the floor. An inch closer to the end? We had travelled that inch, we were at the end.

'You'll sit on my coffin and eat ladoos [Indian sweetmeats],' I remember her saying.

An abridged version of this account, entitled 'A Beginning and an End' appeared in *Right of Way: Prose and Poetry from the Asian Women Writers Collective* (Women's Press, 1988).

The Third Child

Mandy Rose

In memory of Jemima

1982

That summer I was feeling very bad and as if my problems weren't open to help through the advice of friends or my own self-questioning. I felt instead I needed some therapy and opted for psychoanalysis, having for some time been interested in Freud. To find someone to see I wrote to an elderly and respected woman analyst whose writing I had liked. She referred me to another woman with whom I began therapy. The sessions, though troubling, also felt productive and so, as it was August, we talked about my continuing after her summer break which was imminent.

During the last session she said, in response to some remark of mine, something that I remember as, 'It does seem you have some problems with being a woman.' I was outraged. 'I don't have a problem. There IS a problem. Being a woman IS a problem, under Patriarchy.'

It's actually hard for me to believe that this woman made

quite such a clumsy remark, and that may not be exactly what she said. But what interests me here is not so much her remark as my response; that I wasn't prepared to discuss the subject at all. Looking back it seems that feminism was a means of speaking about, and at the same time avoiding, my feelings about being a woman.

Mother

Today, May 1st, was my mother's birthday. My birthday is also this week and as a child I felt that this gave me a special link to her. At my convent junior school May was the month dedicated to Mary. On May day, there we'd be, in our pale-blue-and-white-checked summer dresses, straw boaters, white socks and gloves freshly out of the cupboard, singing,

> *May is the month of Mary,*
> *Month we all love so well,*
> *Mary is God's own mother,*
> *Gladly her praises we tell.*
> *Mary is beautiful, Mary is fair,*
> *Gladly we praise her in song and in prayer.*

The madonna, my own mother, the excitement of the two birthdays, the promise of sunny days; May 1st was the most beautiful day of the year.

Amanda was the third child of professional parents, born into an outer-London household at a time when her father was beginning to enjoy some success in his career. Her mother, who had given up work as an actress during her first pregnancy, had a daughter and a son before Amanda was born, and a daughter and two sons after. Her mother seems to have managed her six children by putting a lot of value on fairness and self-control, but also allowing them quite a bit of freedom and responsibility. Though she liked to see her children looking neat and well-behaved in public, the house had a relaxed feel and she encouraged her children's games and adventures.

Amanda treasures early memories of a rough and tumble family intimacy, where none the less sibling rivalry loomed large and time alone with her parents was rare and precious. Amanda's approach to this problem was to help her mother with the younger children. She found she could get praise and satisfaction by being helpful, grown-up, undemanding.

The taste of Farex, which I would feed to my younger brother on a plastic spoon, the smell of Johnson's Baby Powder, the sight of wrinkled baby legs splashing in the bath.

When I was four I went to nursery school. I can remember Mummy smiling when, at the end of my first day, I told her that the teacher said I was so grown-up that my job there was to help her with the little children.

Father

He made us giggle. He loved to organise games for us to play. He made TV programmes for a living when some girls at school hadn't even got TVs yet. I remember dreaming at age six or so, that he and my older brother were at an award ceremony, receiving their prize for 'winning the War'. I think it must have been the year of the Olympic Games – the ceremony had that kind of look... When I think of the dream I hear the expression 'We won the War' – that's what people used to say.

Her father was a producer at the BBC on the police series Z Cars. He often worked late. But if the children didn't actually see him, they would eagerly watch his name go up last on the credits three nights a week. Sometimes, at weekends, their father would have to attend rehearsals. Amanda's greatest treat was to go with him. There she would revel in the attention she would get, charming the actors and her father, without competition from her siblings and safe from her mother's reproving look.

In junior school there was a running joke about the size of my family and my father's profession. 'Her father's a Producer...' girls would say, when I told someone new that I had five brothers and sisters. I would hate it – wish they hadn't said it. It made him sound like a Lothario, and it made me feel irrelevant – one of his many 'productions'.

Sister

I have two sisters – one whom I have always thought of as 'pretty', the other as 'beautiful'. My friend Leslie says that siblings divide the world between them – one can be clever, one pretty, one good at sport. I guess I was sometimes the 'bright' one, often I was 'helpful', sometimes 'funny'. As far back as I can remember I have felt a failure when it came to looks. In old photos. I can now see how alike my sisters and I actually were as children, also my own particular charm. But the feeling of failure remains.

Among my photos is a picture of my older brother and me, at age ten or so – fishing in the Thames, which ran past the house where we were living at that time. The image pleases me – we look completely engrossed, easy together. Until I was in my early teens I considered my big brother my closest friend. I would spend time with him and his mates – cycling, fishing, hanging around in the park. With my sisters I felt plain, boyish. With the boys I was different – admired. As a tomboy I felt secure about being a girl.

1965

Just before Amanda's eighth birthday, her mother went into hospital to give birth to her sixth child. Amanda herself had been born at home and this hospital birth may have been the first time the children were parted from their mother. Two months later her mother returned to the same hospital, where she was diagnosed as having advanced cancer.

The smell of the hospital; Mummy in bed – so thin, unfamiliar, being looked after. Who looked after us? I don't remember. I don't remember explanations or discussions with Dad. I don't remember being upset. One day walking home from school I thought, 'Maybe she'll die, then they'll feel sorry for me.' I could place myself now exactly on the spot where I had that thought – walking home from school, with the park to my left and the river in sight.

Why, when so much of that time has slipped away, do I remember this? Because I felt guilty to have thought such a thing? Did I recall it after Mummy died and feel responsible? And why did I want people to 'feel sorry for me'? Why was I so hungry for attention – because Mummy was ill, or was this always so in my large family? I don't know. And in the end the memory is all there is – a glimpse of the strong desire of my eight-year-old self to be taken more notice of – a glimpse of ambivalence towards my mother?

In the last weeks of her life Amanda's mother was cared for by a nurse at home. It was Christmas time. Amanda remembers the house seeming cold, quiet. She thinks there were no decorations that year. Before their mother left again to go back to the hospital the children were allowed into the bedroom one by one to see her. Amanda remembers finding her mother ugly, not wanting to kiss her goodbye.

One morning after New Year Dad said he wanted to talk to me, that he had some very bad news. I followed him out into the wintry garden. It was unusual, uncomfortable, to be alone with him. I thought I was prepared for the worst, asking, 'Mummy's going to be in a wheelchair?' 'She's going to have to stay in the hospital?'

After the death of their mother, the children were sent away to their paternal grandmother who lived in Swanage, a seaside town where the family usually went in the summer. Amanda remembers the empty beach, a dead gull, an overwhelming feeling of bleakness. The funeral took place in the children's absence.

Daughter

Amanda first came to see me at the age of twenty-nine. She told me that she had been in therapy briefly before but was awkward about the reasons why she had stopped. She came to see me soon after the end of a long-standing love affair which had left her with feelings of hopelessness about her capacity to love and be loved. She told me she wanted to address the conflicts which she had experienced in regard to her lover, and which had caused her to break

*off the affair. Troubled by her relationship with this man
and with other lovers in the past, she finds that with intimacy come feelings of uncertainty over self-worth, an
inability to express herself freely, and ambivalence regarding the idea of being a wife and mother.*

*Amanda's mother died in January; in early April her father
remarried. His new wife was a divorcee with two children
under five who lived on their street.*

*Two months after her mother's death Amanda says she
watched this woman and her father holding hands in the
garden. Were they in love? She couldn't make it out; her
mother was only just dead so how could he be in love
already? Yet he must be in love to marry, since marriage
must be based on love. Twenty years on she still talks
about this with confusion. How could he do it? Why did he
do it: her father's remarriage seems like a betrayal of her
mother. And a side of her still holds her father up as an
ideal. Other men are unreliable, potential betrayers.*

*Like the funeral, the remarriage took place while Amanda
was away – on holiday with a friend's family. During her
absence, her mother's personal things had been cleared
away, and photos which she was in had been removed.
Amanda felt as if her mother had been violently erased and
was supposed to be forgotten, or at least not mentioned.*

Today I spoke with my father on the phone. I wondered if he
thought of my mother yesterday, remembered her birthday.
But I didn't ask. He thanked me for a letter in which I had
talked of some current difficulties, saying he was glad I'd
written to him about those things. I was stilted, awkward,
changed the subject fast. I always used to see him as the
source of the reticence between us – which stemmed from
the silence I felt he had imposed around my mother's death.

These days I see how I hold back, play my part in keeping a barrier up. My father isn't an easy man – he avoids confrontation, is embarrassed by too much introspection. When I try and picture the time around my mother's illness and death, I imagine him unresponsive, awkward about our sadness, scared to show his own.

Because this lack of communication was negative for me, I value openness. But I see how I stand in the way of it; I brush things off, pretend not to notice problems which scare me, or appear so vulnerable that I silence others, make them fearful of hurting me. I take after my father.

Mother

Amanda's stepmother's first marriage had been stormy and her husband had left her soon after the birth of her second child, disappearing and not providing her with financial support. Alone in suburbia with two small children for a number of years, she didn't hesitate to become the mother of six more children, recently bereaved, one only nine months old.

Her own mother, a dancer, had not got on with her academic husband. While he was away in the army she had had an affair and become pregnant. On his return he divorced her and she left, taking only her youngest daughter, the child of the affair. Amanda's stepmother seems to have completely denied any feelings of rejection by her mother. She identified with her father's second wife. She made it clear to her stepchildren that she saw no particular virtue in natural mothers or first marriages.

At first I was excited about my new mother. She was 'modern' – she wore her hair in a plait, had Beatles records and cooked pasta. We called her by her first name. She had been to a progressive public school not so far from where we lived. I applied and won a scholarship to go there. I wanted to be close to her. But it wasn't easy. She gave very obvious preference to her own children. I tried not to mind, telling myself it was understandable.

Then there was the housework. She made it clear she felt over-burdened with it. And there was a lot to be done; with her two children, my brothers and sisters, and soon a new baby. She complained about it but very often refused help. Her resentment began to dominate the house.

Amanda would alternate between an attitude of hopeful communicativeness and a depressive silence. During many sessions in the first year she would cry for much of the time without being able to talk about the thoughts and feelings which accompanied the tears. This difficulty with express- ing herself was the cause of a great deal of frustration to her.

As for her relationship to me – transference love was pre- sent very soon. She had recurring dreams in which we were intimate friends, sharing confidences. One day, having encountered me on the street, she told me that she had thought, 'Maybe she is my mother.'

Her fear of rejection takes a number of forms. She con- sistently arrives late, to be sure to find me waiting for her. She hesitates to broach new areas, wanting my approval. She is very reluctant to express anger or aggression, or not to appear 'nice'. She defends herself against this possibility with silence.

Amanda would like to have a child, but is terrified of motherhood. One day she said, 'I think I'd just die if I was not working, if I was a housewife, at home with a baby.'

During my teenage years the tension at home became acute.

There was a proliferation of rules, often unspoken. Books belonging to my stepmother weren't to be taken off the shelves. One must be available to help with meals, but shouldn't ask what time they'd be. Rooms, once cleaned, had to be left untouched. On one occasion Dad sneezed in the laundry room and all the clothes on the line were washed again. Such things weren't mentioned. Sometimes Dad would give me a lift to school. I would dread this time alone with him as there would be an uncomfortable silence between us. I guess I felt we must speak about the intolerable situation, about HER.

Amanda compares the world of her teenage home to that of a prison. The children divided into those who were in favour and those who were not. It was dangerous to associate with those who were out of favour, who were known to harbour critical thoughts. Amanda was torn. Wanting affection, she tried to please her stepmother, while feeling like a traitor to her siblings.

Amanda's father plays a minor role in her account of that time. She depicts him, like the children, as a victim of circumstances, in no way responsible for what happened in the family. She says he never intervened in the difficulties between his second wife and his children. He would work late, and often stay away. When he was at home Amanda says he would pretend not to notice his wife's coldness, or try to win her over with humour. Amanda speaks of this with evident anger.

I lived with my stepmother for ten years, longer than I lived with my mother. We are not in touch now. Like my mother she lives for me as memory, as fantasy.

About a year after leaving home, at the age of nineteen, I read Germaine Greer's *The Female Eunuch*. It had a dramatic effect on me. It spoke to a cluster of thoughts and feelings which I didn't even know I had and had no language for. I poured these feelings into feminism. I became active in women's politics, then joined the Communist Party and became women's organiser of my branch.

In my teens I had been awkward about how to present myself. Dressing in a 'girlish' way felt all wrong. I half expected people to laugh at me, mock my attempts. Make-up didn't help. I couldn't seem to do it well and would feel self-conscious about the evidence that I was trying to improve things. I was relieved when I found a boyfriend who was keen on the 'natural look'. Now I didn't have to worry; it was 'correct' to feel unwilling to be an object for the male gaze. I took to wearing workmen's dungarees and Doc Martens, and hennaed my cropped hair.

I became attracted by an idea of emotional independence. I would begin relationships with men, but withdraw when certain uncomfortable feelings arose; telling myself these had to do with them, not me.

It's not that I didn't see any inter-relationship between my politics and my personal history. I did. I would talk about my stepmother's unhappiness with being a wife and mother as symptomatic of women's situation. Meanwhile part of me thought of her more as a tyrant than a victim...

In the light of my feminism I would sometimes think about my mother, wish that I knew more about her. But I didn't think about it the other way round, consider what kind of a daughter she had produced in me, and what impact her death and the events that followed from it might have had on my feelings about being a girl. It was a number of years before I began to question what these things might have to do with my strength of feeling about power relations between men and women, about femininity, about the positions of wife and mother. In situating all the 'ills' for women in the external world, I was protected from the possibility that I might in fact have particular conflicts about being a woman and that my receptiveness to feminism had to do, in part, with finding a repository for unconscious feelings.

I told my therapist that my mother died of cervical cancer. The summer after my mother died, my best friend's mother died, of breast cancer. First my mother, then hers, so soon after – women's cancers. Her mother had a mastectomy. I listened to talk of tumours, spreading cancers, imagined the hole left after a breast was gone.

While I was writing this piece I spoke with my older sister about our mother's illness. I was taken aback to find that she understood her to have had not cervical but stomach cancer. For twenty-five years I have attributed my mother's death to a 'feminine' cause. In recent years I had come to see this as the source of my nervousness about being a mother myself. Now I find that to have been a fantasy, on the part of my tomboy, eight-year-old self. It was a confusing discovery; as if part of me was founded on an illusion.

Yesterday I had supper with Karen, Tricia and Naomi. Exchanging news about work, families, I realised that three of the four of us are in the same profession as our fathers. The thought touched me. We'd met ten or more years ago, in our early twenties – feminists, newly free of our families, determined to make different lives from those of our parents. We had been close friends while making decisions about training and careers. And now I see how unfree in one sense those choices were, how determined by what was familiar to us in childhood.

Feminists have been accused of being male-identified, uncomfortable with being women. But what is femininity for us? The world of work for many of my generation of English middle-class children was the masculine world, the world of the father. Becoming adult women has meant fol-

lowing in our fathers' footsteps – our career choices shaped
by a complex of Oedipal and political desire, and social
change.

1988

I dreamt I met my mother – the only time I remember
dreaming about her. In the dream she hadn't died but had
gone to live in America.

My lover at that time was American. He has the same
name as my father, so of course I had sometimes wondered
about the connections between those two men, for me. But
in the dream it's my mother who is in the place of my lover,
she's 'in America'.

We were involved for seven years. I would visit him as
often as I could, or we would meet up somewhere.
Sometimes I would get to stay with him for a while – for
two, three months. For a long time it felt OK to me. I would
miss him when we were apart, but not so badly that it really hurt. Instead, I'd be buoyed up by knowing that he was
there, that he loved me, as he did, passionately, reliably. For
his own reasons, it suited him too, though he found the sep-
arations more painful. His absence didn't seem intolerable.
I had lived with the idea of an absent loved one. It was
familiar to me.

He is a child therapist; he looks after children, maternal.
But he is also father-like. As well as the shared name, he is
somewhat older than me, wears suits, ties. A kind of repa-
ration; to find a fatherly man whose very occupation
announces him as a man who makes up for my father's failure – who looks after children, specifically, talks to children
about their difficulties.

But things weren't perfect. When we would get together,

it could be difficult. There would be silences, which I couldn't break and couldn't bear. I would get tongue-tied. While I had withdrawn from previous boyfriends, he wouldn't let me. He would sit it out, trying to let me know that the silences had to be more painful than whatever it was they were designed to cloak. Sometimes this worked, and I would be happy, and very much in love with him. But these crises would recur, and we both grew tired of having to struggle with them. It would be a relief to be alone again. When the relationship ended I found a professional therapist.

One Christmas, a couple of years after he and my stepmother finally separated, my father gave us each a little package of family photos. Apart from occasional and nerve-wracking raids into his desk over the years, I hadn't looked at photos of my mother, or of my own childhood.

Rather sweetly, it seemed to me, he had made selections so that each of us had a package tending to feature ourselves. In my photos, I am the one on whom my father smiles adoringly, or I am alone in the frame. Six sets of photos, in which a different child plays the starring role.

The photos are mainly of holidays – camping in Brittany, and in Wales, group shots on unidentifiable beaches, black and white, sun shining down the lens. A kind of *Swallows and Amazons* atmosphere – this gang of children, tanned, hair bleached from the sun. I am filled with nostalgia. I imagine if Mummy had lived, my fantasies about the 'golden days' of early childhood would have been tempered somewhat by later events, and by her recollections of that time. As it is I think of my childhood in two 'chapters' – the good, sunny times before Mummy died, and the bad, grey times after.

In the photos my mother tends to appear in fifties cotton dresses, playdex sandals, espadrilles, baggy jumpers – the kinds of things I wear now. I have always been attracted to fifties clothes and designs – looking at the photos, I recognise these as the shapes and styles of my childhood.

Lately, I've taken to wearing lipstick, as I see in the photos my mother often did. It has everything to do with her; the way it smells reminds me of her dressing table, the colour I wear she might have worn. Once in a while when I catch sight of my reflection I am taken aback; I see my mother's face in mine. It's a little spooky. But it's also OK. I see myself as a woman, her daughter.

Postscript

Reading this piece I was struck by the third-person voice, the voice of the therapist, which pleased me. It occurred to me that this point of view had helped me to write, let me feel a little more detached from painful material. It also allowed me to command attention, to tell my story, while not feeling self-indulgent in the way an insistent 'I' made me feel. In creating this voice I think I was very much my mother's daughter – not wanting to appear too demanding. And I think that my mother is present in this voice in another respect, too. I like the sound of this voice – it's sympathetic, non-judgmental. It knows all about me. It is the voice of an ideal mother – a voice of unconditional love.

Thanks to Leslie Dick, Paul Gilroy, Andrea Fraser, Kate Pullinger, Karen Whiteson and Vron Ware.

Autumn 1980

Marilyn Hacker

I spent the night after my mother died
in a farmhouse north of Saratoga Springs
belonging to a thirty-nine-year-old
professor with long, silvered wiry hair,
a lively girl's flushed cheeks and gemstone eyes.
I didn't know that she had died.
Two big bitches and a varying
heap of cats snoozed near a black wood stove
on a rag rug, while, on the spring-shot couch
we talked late over slow glasses of wine.
In the spare room near Saratoga Springs
was a high box-bed. My mother died
that morning, of heart failure, finally.
Insulin shocks burned out her memory.
On the bed, a blue early-century
Texas Star, in a room white and blue
as my flannel pajamas. I'd have worn
the same, but smaller, ten years old at home.
Home was the Bronx, on Eastburn Avenue,
miles south of the hermetic not-quite-new
block where they'd sent this morning's ambulance.

Her nurse had telephoned. My coat was on,
my book-stuffed bag already on my back.
She said, 'Your mother had another shock.
We'll be taking her to the hospital.'
I asked if I should stay. She said, 'It's all
right.' I named the upstate college where
I'd speak that night. This had happened before.
I knew/I didn't know: it's not the same.
November cold was in that corner room
upstairs, with a frame window over land
the woman and another woman owned
—who was away. I thought of her alone
in her wide old bed, me in mine. I turned
the covers back. I didn't know she had died.
The tan dog chased cats; she had to be tied
in the front yard while I went along
on morning errands until, back in town,
I'd catch my bus. November hills were raw
fall after celebratory fall
foliage, reunions, festival.
I blew warmth on my hands in a dark barn
where two shaggy mares whuffled in straw,
dipped steaming velvet muzzles to the pail
of feed. We'd left the pick-up's heater on.
It smelt like kapok when we climbed inside.
We both unzipped our parkas for the ride
back to the Saratoga bus station.
I blamed the wind if I felt something wrong.
A shrunken-souled old woman whom I saw
once a month lay on a hospital
slab in the Bronx. Mean or not, that soul
in its cortege of history was gone.
I didn't know that I could never know,
now the daughtering magic to recall

across two coffee-mugs the clever Young
Socialist whose views would coincide
with mine. I didn't know that she had died.
Not talking much, while weighted sky pressed down,
we climbed the back road's bosom to the
all-night diner doubling as a bus depot.
I brushed my new friend's cool cheek with my own,
and caught the southbound bus from Montreal.
I counted boarded-up racetrack motel
after motel. I couldn't read. I tried
to sleep. I didn't know that she had died.
Hours later, outside Port Authority,
rained on, I zipped and hooded an obscure
ache from my right temple down my shoulder.
Anonymous in the mid-afternoon
crowds, I'd walk, to stretch, I thought, downtown.
I rode on the female wave, typically
into Macy's (where forty-five years
past, qualified by her new MA
in Chemistry, she'd sold Fine Lingerie),
to browse in Fall Sale bargains for my child,
aged six, size eight, hung brilliantly or piled
like autumn foliage I'd missed somehow,
and knew what I officially didn't know
and put the bright thing down, scalded with tears.

Cravings

Shirley P. Cooper

It was strange / when the nurse announced / the forthcoming event / I wanted to tell you / but you weren't here / I wanted to be told / I was too young / inexperienced / making a mistake / I wanted to share my happiness with you / I wanted hints to survive / I wanted you to tell me how you felt as you carried me / how your body changed / how your relationship with my father came about / what he said when you told him you were expecting / why he left you to cope / why my sister has the same first name /
I wanted to know why Papa disapproved / did you crave mangoes / bananas / ice-cream / and love / did you cry as you told him / did you try to protect your feelings by telling him you'd manage with or without him / how did you feel as you looked at your swelling belly / did you wake him in the night to go and get you some ice-cream or a Chinese / did you leave two pounds of bananas by the side of the bed / in case you got hungry or did you leave the opened tin of fruits with a spoon in /

*do you remember the days you cried for no apparent
reason / the feelings of loneliness and aloneness / or
the extremely happy days when everyone else looked
sad / did you eat out of the pot because the plate was-
n't big enough / how many times did the child inside
you jump to remind you that: where there's life
there's hope / I hear he went for the midwife when
you were in labour and came back for the christening /
is it true that there was a war between Dominica, St
Kitts and Anguilla that day / did I jump inside you at
his presence / when he said if you a de muma an e
kick you so imagine wha e would do wid me / were
you hurt when you felt like a second cousin to a bus /
did he tell you that he loved you / did he flaunt his
non-pregnant girlfriend in front of you / did you yearn
for his touch in those nine months /
would you believe that although I've never known
you / I had a similar experience / twenty-six years
later /
Time / would I have done the same if I knew you'd
done it!*

The Other Mother

Shireen Sheikh

I hated you for abandoning me. I'll never forgive you. I was seventeen when you left me defenceless, your daughter.

But I had the other mother, the sister who stayed.

How could you have been so selfish? You saw things in the short term, always wanting to get out, to evade, avoid.

And when you died, your other daughter became my other mother.

Was it so impossible to start again? Daddy was gone, the debts were large, the house had been repossessed. Was there really nowhere to go when you took your life?

My other mother took me in. Oedipus Revisited. I remembered how I'd hated her husband. Not for the sex. But for the money, for the power.

Dead in the bed, you had no power. A discarded bottle

emptied of its lethal pills, a note ('Forgive me') clutched in your frozen hand, your face wearing its mask of triumph. Tortured and tormented, you had no space for the living.

My other mother wants me to live. She was there for me when I was studying for my 'A' levels. She saw me through university. She used her contacts to find me a job. She was there for me.

You were never there for me. I was the daughter who wasn't the son.

My other mother told me to write. She would even give me money when I couldn't cover all the bills. I don't know how she could afford it. Her husband was ill, they were running up huge debts, soon they wouldn't be able to meet the mortgage repayments. History Repeats.

You're dead and gone. This is half the story.

Sometimes when the moon is full I want to die. Like my other mother.

What a legacy you left us.

Paralysis

Susan Ardill

My experience of my mother's death was a very complicated one. So many stories unravelling at the same time – the story of my mother's death, of me and my mother, of Australia and England, of my relationship with Penny and my love affair with Wendy, of my brother and sisters and the realignment of the family, of the other deaths, Catherine and Kim, and of Catholicism and psychoanalysis. Nothing happened alone, and it's hard to describe such a gale-force experience.

I could tell you, in fact I want to tell you but I have to restrain myself, every detail of the events of those days. Details are important when people die – what time it was when you heard, what they said the day before, how hot it was at the graveside. When my mother died I needed to know everything, and my sisters and brother and I loved to talk over everything about her and her death every day in the weeks that followed. It's all stored inside me and when I tell people bits of the story I want to quiz them afterwards to make sure they took everything in in the right order and appreciated its full meaning. In reality I've given up on this, because I've realised this is my own obsession with the facts, hoping those facts will one day reveal a meaning which will make everything smooth and OK. I also know now that they won't and I go along through life with both that expectation of resolution and the knowledge of its impossibility held inside me side by side.

So, here are the bare bones of the story.

My mother died quite suddenly in January 1988. She was sixty-three years old and I was thirty-one at the time. I was living in London but I'm Australian and she and the rest of my family were living in Sydney. After a basically heartless marriage, my father had moved out some years before, and Mum lived with my youngest sister. My mother had been a paraplegic, confined to a wheelchair, for eleven years before she died. She was discovered to have benign tumours on her spine when I was fourteen, and the rest of my teenage years saw her having a series of major operations, long stays in rehabilitation hospitals, her walking gradually deteriorating, until she went into a wheelchair when I was twenty.

Illness, hospitals, doctors and medical paraphernalia were a part of everyday life for me in relation to my mother. So when people ask, 'Did your mother die suddenly?', it's hard to know what to say. It was at once a shock and yet not the unthinkable.

She went into hospital to have a very routine operation to clean out a persistent bedsore, an occupational hazard for people in wheelchairs. After the operation she didn't recover from the anaesthetic very well, was dozy and slept a lot. The doctors were concerned and were doing tests, but three days after the operation, while my brother was sitting with her, she suddenly stopped breathing. If she hadn't been in hospital, she would have died at that time, but of course medical teams raced to her side, she was rushed to intensive care, revived, and put on life-support systems. But she never regained consciousness and slipped away gradually, dying three days later. (It turned out that she had grown more tumours on the lining of her brain, which had started bleeding under the influence of the anaesthetic, eventually affecting the respiratory centre in her brain.)

The doctors realised she was unsaveable soon after her original respiratory arrest. Certainly when my brother rang me in London a couple of hours later he was already able to tell me that she was definitely going to die. It was a strange sort of reprieve, to be told that my mother had not quite died but was going to. I felt glad really, to have that period of transition and adjustment. It helped to know that she was still there, still existing on the other side of the world, even if only for a while. The outcome was inevitable, but at least when I got the news her death was not a complete *fait accompli*.

The most significant thing about hearing of my mother's death, and this is impossible to convey, is the total newness of that news. The body reacts by breathing faster, by feeling weak and shocked (but not by crying for some time), the mind is in a new place, everything is changed. Precisely a year earlier my close friend Kim had been killed in a motorbike accident – I also received news of her death by phone from Australia, felt the panic and shock. But that moment of news of my mother's death was something else, some massive alteration in the way things were and were ever going to be. All this was felt in the first few minutes.

My reaction was that I would go to Australia, there was no question of not doing that. A year before Kim's death, my first lover (and first love) Catherine had also died, of the cumulative effects of drug abuse. So it felt to me as though people close to me kept dying, disappearing. But, from London, I had no way of measuring their absence, or making it visible in my life. I'd had to struggle with those other two deaths mostly in private. This time it had to be different, because it was my mother, and also I think because on some level all the frustrated energy of the past two years' attempts to make sense of death coalesced, so that I felt possessed of the most tremendous nervous energy. From the moment of my mother's death, and especially during the following three weeks which I spent in Australia, I actively wanted to do the hard emotional and sometimes physical labour her death necessitated. I didn't want to avoid anything. I was driven by her death, I wanted to feel and go through it all, I had to see that she was really gone. And while I was seeing that she was dead, Kim and Catherine were always at the back of my mind too.

The experience of Mum's death stands out in dramatic relief in my life, even more than it might ordinarily, because I had to fly halfway round the world to take part in it. Which is very different from having it mixed in with day-to-day life. That discrepancy between my experience and the rest of the family's was confusing. I think I welcomed the drama of that global flight because it concentrated my energy, because the whole event stood out as special, with different colours and sights and participants than my usual life in England. That specialness seemed appropriate, I needed something big to mark the momentousness of what had happened. At the same time I felt guilty, and was resented by my family, because I largely didn't have to deal with the mundane details which always follow death and take so long to clear up. I was also scared, worried that living in London had cushioned me from the abrupt and severe pain of having someone taken out of my life in a direct way, from right in front of me. Guilty that I didn't suffer enough? Even though I thought I had renounced guilt along with Catholicism when I was eighteen, 1988 made me think again.

There is another story which ran parallel to my mother's death and which for me was an enormous part of it. By a

strange coincidence, the timing of her death had very particular consequences for me. Once I might have imagined
that you would step out of your own aberrant, subcultural
life into some pure and loving, familial response to mother's
death. That you stopped being whoever else you are and just
became the daughter. That didn't happen.

For four of the six years I'd been living in London I'd been
in a relationship with Penny, who had been to Australia
with me and met my mother and was a very significant
lover, although we didn't live together. But for the last six
months our relationship had turned quite difficult and distant, bouncing from good to bad times. Perhaps it was a
measure of our estrangement that I'd recently started a
light-hearted flirtation with another woman, Wendy, someone I barely knew and rarely saw. However, on a winter's
night in London, the night of my mother's operation in
Sydney, I ran into Wendy, she suggested dinner, and we
ended up spending the night together. It's hard to describe
the lightning effect this had on me. I remember lying in bed
while she slept and thinking 'Who is this extraordinary and
lovely person?' It felt like an angel had dropped into my life.
Right from that unexpected beginning I guess it was clear
she was going to be important to me.

Of course I had to tell Penny about this but over the following weekend events conspired to prevent us from being
alone together until the Sunday. But still I didn't tell her...
trying to avoid conflict, I suppose. We were having a nice
time, I was really exhausted and couldn't face some traumat-
ic discussion of the fact that I'd slept with somebody else. I
was putting off the confession, unable to know what consequences that would have. I stayed at Penny's place on Sunday
night and in the morning she'd literally just gone down the
stairs to leave for work when the phone rang. I picked it up –
it was my brother ringing from Australia saying that Mum

had had a respiratory arrest and that she was going to die. It was like a bomb going off. Immediately I was swept into the chaos of that news. Yet in all the franticness of the next few hours, I couldn't completely put aside my preoccupation with Wendy. In fact I decided to fly to Sydney three days later rather than the very next day, because even in the light of my mother dying I absolutely had to see her again.

All the elements of the drama which was to engulf me for the next year were present in that first half hour after the phone call, but there was no way I could have dissected them then. Penny said, 'I'll come to Australia too, do you want me to come?' And I said 'Yes', while having a faint sense that this was the wrong decision. Somewhere my mind registered that this offer of Penny's, in the light of our recently troubled relationship, carried a big gesture of commitment towards a future together. Unknown to her, I had done something which maybe threatened that future. Yet at that moment how could I weigh the love and familiarity of our four years against one night? At that point I was incapable of rationality or strength of mind. My need was so crushing, I accepted all that was offered to me. I felt it was completely impossible and inappropriate to tell Penny about Wendy. It seemed as though the discourse between us would then change from 'What do you feel about your mother dying?' to 'What is the nature of our relationship and how could you do this to me?' By that decision I now see I was placing her in the position of supporter, rather than lover, to me. I deceived her, and I believe she's never forgiven me for that.

It's taken me almost four years even to be able to describe succinctly what the ingredients of my dilemma were. At the time, there was no dilemma, there were only huge blocks of feeling and impulses which drove me in contradictory directions. I let Penny come to Australia to be at my side at my mother's funeral, while carrying on a secret affair which fal-

sified my relationship with her. For months afterward I flag-
ellated myself for being such a weakling. But it was a revelation to me that I could be so weak, that I could have the
ground swept from under me, that I could be unable to anal-
yse or act with integrity according to a cogent view of the
situation. For ages I felt like I had tainted my mother's death
with this deception, that I myself was tainted. It took me a
long time to be able to see how my behaviour then was
explicable, how it arose from the past, my past with Penny
and with my mother. That's another story.

The day after my brother's phone call I arranged for
Wendy, who was working till one in the morning, to come
to my place after work. At midnight the phone call come
from my brother and sisters in Australia saying that my
mother had finally died. So Wendy was the first person I saw
after I got that news. At this very intimate moment in my
life I spent the night with a virtual stranger. We stayed up
until about five in the morning talking about childhood. My
mind was on the edge of spinning off somewhere very
frightening, but Wendy was a warm and vital connection.
All the time I kept thinking, 'This is so strange.' I could picture my brother and sisters in Australia: it was the middle
of summer, they would all be at the house, with my mother's family, being upset together and doing things like making funeral arrangements. Meanwhile, here I was in bed
with a strange woman in England. I suppose I must have had
a residue of guilt about being a lesbian or being sexual at all.
Abstractly, it seemed inappropriate and even disrespectful.
In reality, I was immersed in an almost painful sensuality
which seemed absolutely necessary and right. I kept thinking, 'My mother's dead, my mother's dead,' and next to that
thinking, 'This is my life, here in this bed in this woman's
arms I'm alive and this is the place I want to be and the best
possible thing I could be doing.'

I suppose what I've realised since then, and it's something else that evokes guilt, is that some of the function of the sexual excitement was to lessen the pain of my mother's death. Certainly her death was a very heavy blow, but in the months that followed I had a passion which energised me and heightened all my senses and which was an outlet for my feelings about her. Sex and death, what a cliché, and yet I lived it.

So I flew off to Australia. The next three weeks were filled with activity – seeing mother's body, the Catholic funeral and wake, visiting her friends. I went to the hospital on my own to collect some of Mum's things and had to push her empty wheelchair with her handbag on it out and down the road. Crying of course. Every morning I woke early and cried for a couple of hours. At that point it was clean and easy grief – the hard stuff starts later. I felt at once manic and worn out. Usually, on previous visits home to Australia, I'd found it a strain to stay at the family home out in the suburbs, wanting to be with my friends in the alternative world of the inner city. But this time I could hardly function away from home – I felt exhausted and depleted if I went out for more than a couple of hours – I wanted to get back to the house to be replenished. I had to be near my mother's things and the place where she'd spent so much time.

I have many sensual memories of those weeks. I remember a few days after the funeral going rowing on a river just a half mile from the cemetery, lying in the boat looking up at the surrounding tall gum trees, thinking about Mum's body in the coffin in the ground not far away.

Another time I was at a friend's house, lying alone on the floor in the twilight. I was overcome with the sensation that my mother was not in the world anymore – that she had existed all of my life and before that, and now she didn't. It was a very primitive feeling.

Penny and I were very close and she was included in the

family group throughout our stay. An exchange of cards was the only contact I had with Wendy. But as my return flight approached, I thought about her more. My excitement about her had not lessened. Penny decided to stay on in Sydney for a week or two longer than me. Still I didn't tell her about my infidelity. I just couldn't bear the consequences.

So I came back to England alone and commenced a passionate affair. That in itself was strange, at once to feel heavily depressed and sunk in thoughts about the death, and then to be intoxicated with this new person. When Penny came back two weeks later I finally had to tell her. So complete were my defences against the meaning of what I'd done, that I was surprised when she took it as a betrayal and attack upon her. Literally within minutes of my telling her that I'd slept with somebody else, she declared our relationship categorically over. For the most part she then refused to see me.

I didn't know how to deal with such an absolute response from Penny. I kept wanting to see and talk to her. For months I oscillated wildly between the pull to my known and cherished relationship and everything that we'd shared together and the pull to the new relationship that was exciting and full of life. A common story, of course, but for me it meant that simultaneous with the loss of my mother was the loss of everything familiar which had made up my life in London. I lost Penny and all the memories and associations we held in common, which told me who I was. And I lost the only person in England who'd been there at the funeral and with my family. So totally did she cut off from me, it was almost like the fourth death. It wasn't till late in the year that I accepted that the relationship was over; partly I struggled against that realisation because it was mixed up with accepting that Mum was dead, that something was gone and finished.

If my mother had not died, would Penny have accepted me having an affair? Our four and a half years together had not been totally monogamous. Penny insisted that her reaction was completely in response to my deception, rather than my sexual unfaithfulness itself. I suspected that in this case that wasn't true, but I was in no position to argue for leniency in the face of such a damning judgement.

If Penny hadn't rejected me so absolutely, would I have become so involved with Wendy? I kicked and kicked against what seemed like inevitability – I couldn't accept that the choice had been taken out of my hands by a simple twist of fate, that Mum's death could be so instrumental in determining what path my life went down.

When I look back at 1988 I see it as just a storm of feelings. The initial impact of her death lasted the whole year. All of that time that peculiar combination of mania and exhaustion stayed with me. I had the strange sensation of not having slept properly since the death. It felt like there was some part of my brain which never shut down, so that even if I'd slept ten hours I wasn't refreshed. Superficially it appeared that I was sleeping reasonably OK, but it was a long time before I felt truly rested again.

Very soon after I came back to England I commenced psychoanalysis. Mum's death was a rupture so deep that I had no choice except to plunge into it. There were so many things to consider and I could never separate one strand of meaning from another. For example, if I was angry at Penny for taking herself away from me at the time when I most needed some understanding, was that really only because I was angry at Mum for dying? I couldn't be sure of anything. I felt like I was hurtling around, glimpsing thousands of possibilities. This craziness had more than a touch of exhilaration in it – the immediacy of the actions, decisions, feelings required of me made me feel in touch with the elements of existence. Everything felt pared down to the essentials. Alongside the confusion and pain, I also felt a sense of release and excitement. Mum's death, and the psychoanalytic process which I entered into wholeheartedly, freed me from the set understandings I'd held till then. The most deep-seated sense of who I was and my place in the world was up for grabs.

Much of the energy and stimulation which drove me that year arose from my relationship with Wendy. It would have been easy to become attached to anyone at that time who was prepared to listen and sympathise. I was very guarded in case that was all there was to it. Instead, as I realised more clearly in retrospect, over the course of that year our relationship grew directly in response to each new stage in my working out things about Mum's death, about how I wanted my own life to proceed:

1

Wendy was born one of twins, but her brother had died the day after birth. I think out of that she became, within her family and in the world, almost twice as alive, twice as joyful about life, offering double of herself to the world. I would have found that attractive anyway because of the history of negativity and illness within my own family, but because I came across her at the point that my mother died, her vibrancy was especially compelling for me, literally a lifeline. I was possessed by raw ideas about life and death for that whole year of 1988, and to have someone who made me laugh a lot, who made me feel really joyful, well, I just felt released into pleasure in being alive.

Embracing that pleasure was a direct and, as I strongly felt, necessary response to what seemed the overwhelming frustration and suffering of my mother's life. Right from the moment she died my major preoccupation was with the meaning of her life – or rather, what seemed to me to be its meaninglessness. After all, she'd had over thirty years in a bleak, emotionally brutal marriage, then developed a physical condition that trapped and paralysed her for the last decade of her life. Talk about illness as metaphor, well, paralysis was an incredibly neat symbol for the condition of my mother's life and its impact on mine.

My mother had a vitality which, throughout my childhood, was increasingly inhibited by my father's disapproval. In response to his scorn she was almost totally passive. Following her example, none of us stood up to his bullying. The family was a model of compliance and rigidly contained anger. Economically dependent, living as she did within a Catholic subculture where separation and divorce were unknown, she turned her feelings inside, distanced even from her children. Just at the point where maybe she could have hoped for something better, some sort of escape route because her children were growing up, she developed tumours which took away her mobility, which eventually paralysed her.

I couldn't find any material there for a feminist martyrisation. My mother only seemed to have conveyed to me, her daughter, the utmost passivity, masochism and hopelessness.

None of these thoughts was totally new. All my adult feminist life I'd been preoccupied with my relationship to my mother, thinking about how it had influenced the sort of woman I was. At the point of her death it suddenly seemed desperately important to be able to come up with some sort of positive summary of her life, but all I could see were the depressing elements. One of the things that psychoanalysis enabled me to grasp a long time later was how my preoccupation with how 'awful' her life had been was a defence against the fear and pain which came from my unconscious belief that I had caused her illness, that I was the source of her troubles. It was only after the initial frenzy wore off that I was able to see how the way I reacted to her death was intrinsically revealing about the most significant aspects of my relationship to her.

Just over a year after her death I went on a visit back to Australia, which marked some sort of closure to that first intense period. I remember after I'd been there for a few days having the most incredible sensation that Sydney was empty. The city seemed bleak, vacant, there was nothing, no one, there. I could make the connection intellectually with my mother's absence, but that didn't really dispel the power of the projection. Usually I loved going back to Sydney and considered it my home, but this time all those feelings were reversed and I was pleased to come back to London. It seems that my return visit to Australia marked some sort of resolution, maybe it really sank in then that Mum was dead and everything was changed. Back in London, I was full of happiness and energy and my life seemed to surge forward. Then began the longer-term unfolding of the impact of her death.

2

It's ironic that it was not the deaths of two friends of my own age, but my mother's death, at sixty-three, that shocked me into the realisation that I too was eventually going to die. That was no longer an abstract recognition, it became an everyday awareness. Her death panicked me – if that was all there was for her, if she had no more chances to change, to make her life different, then I was sure going to make certain that I didn't lose any opportunities to do everything that my mother hadn't.

Maybe it wasn't dramatically visible to my friends, but internally I was bolder, less tolerant of bullshit, living more in the here and now, rather than rehearsing for something better in the future. I was very conscious of mortality, not fearfully, but in a way that felt productive, creative. This is it, I kept thinking, this is my only chance to do this, to be alive now and feel this.

So much of that sprang from comparison with my mother's stifled life. When someone has died you can suddenly look at their life as a finished story. After you take in the terrible, simple fact that they are dead, your attention gets drawn backwards across their whole lifespan. Like mental time travelling, I find I alight at different moments of my mother's life and look them over. Because her life has ended, I can see it more clearly as a historical entity. I can see that, yes, she was born into that small Australia of the 1920s, had a sheltered and happy girlhood, worked and dated soldiers through the Second World War, married and spent the fifties having babies. Because I can see her life as a story, I get glimpses of my own as one – as a story which may well be halfway through now, as hers was at my age. I was the baby who that particular woman conceived and brought up in a family house on the outskirts of Sydney in the fifties. Now I'm the same age as the Mum who inhabits my earliest memories. My life is beyond her imagination, but my imagination is still fixed on her life.

Direct comparison between my experiences and the outward shape of Mum's life infused my thinking for a year or two after her death. Then that gave way to something more subjective and internal. What remains mostly unseen by the people around me is how much of my mother persists in me. In a way death only changed the appearance of things. If anything, losing her from external life meant I could turn my attention inwards and see how insistently she is present in my psyche, as someone I react to and against. My mother saturates my mind, like a background colour, a colour I don't always realise I'm seeing. Psychoanalysis helps me to see her, and to force my way past her when I need to.

Sometimes it feels as though she is behind everything, every association and intonation. It's as though I'm carrying her in my body just as she did for me once. Who is this woman, who is mother?

I know from theory, but I can't actually imagine, how she was the first person, she was everything in the world to me as an infant. With the help of analysis, I try and piece together what it meant that she was the one who fed and touched me, who smiled at me and filled all my senses. What did she do, or not do, that left me so prone to terrible anxiety?

Then there's the actual Mum I remember, from the mundane world of childhood and teenage years. I silently loved her, felt responsible for her worry and depletion. She was a physically conscientious caretaker but gave me very little emotionally.

There's also that third, feminist, awareness of her role as mother, as family workhorse, and repository of all feelings, the impossibility of that position.

Now as an adult woman, it's as though all three incarnations of mother are present and active, ongoing influences which surround me. I have to keep working hard to recognise them. I have to be constantly on the lookout so that the mother who persists in my psyche does not constrict me, distort my capacity to live as I want.

3

The further away her life gets the more clearly I see how it hangs over mine. Almost four years after her death, her life still yields wave after wave of emotional difficulties for me to swim through. And I am still immersed in the psychoanalytic process, my understanding about it all unfolds very slowly.

I still have to struggle with the meaning of her tumours.

At firsthand I watched her regress to having a baby's wobbly legs, saw the discomfort and degradation brought about by something internal. Why does that happen to anyone, why did that happen to my mother?

It's not just an abstract question of meaning. Now I realise that because of what happened to her, I expect imminent disaster in my own life; I live all the time with an expectation just below the surface that awful things will happen, either to me or to people I love.

I have a barely contained hysteria about my own body and disease which I'm only just becoming conscious of. I find it hard to respond when people close to me are injured or sick. I expect their need to be overwhelming, like hers was.

I've been through periods of emotional paralysis where I unwittingly mimic the condition of Mum's life. I restrict myself to the house, sink into inertia while feeling terribly claustrophobic and trapped.

I always need escape routes, because she didn't have one.

Every so often it strikes me that one of the determining factors in my life is my struggle to separate from her, to leave her behind, to surpass her. Then I fear her anger, her retaliation (from inside of me). I fear that my achievements are a condemnation of her, underline the meaningless of her life. I wonder whether I've curtailed myself on her behalf.

Of course, I've drawn a one-dimensional picture. Neither my mother nor her situation was so relentlessly desolate. She was also outgoing, resilient, a keen follower of politics and local gossip. She had lots of friends.

Neither am I someone who is so dogged by this malevolent ghost that I have no desires or achievements of my own. I am clearly unlike my mother in most ways, and similar to her in some ways that don't trouble me.

All that is true. But still one of the hardest aspects of my mother's death to deal with, to admit to, is what a relief it was to me, and how it continues to be so.

I think she did suffer from an immense depression about what had happened to her. Her tragedy stared us in the face and was a weight around our lives. I felt responsible for making her unhappy, for failing to make her happy. I can only guess that had my mother lived, throughout my thirties this would have remained the same, I would have lived with the burden of her unhappiness. I used to get furious at my mother for not fighting hard enough against her condition. It seemed as though she gave up, bit by bit. I was exasperated by her defeatism. It seemed a slap in the face. I felt endlessly guilty for not encouraging her enough, yet I knew that encouragement was beside the point. My mother and I were stuck in being unable to talk about what we simply felt about what was happening to her. I resented being called upon to care for her, when she had effectively abandoned me when I was fourteen. None of this was ever voiced of course – it came out in a million and one minor spats and silences.

Is it too simplistic now to see my fury as displaced anger about her previous 'paralysis': her inability to leave my father? It's as though my whole life I wanted to scream at her 'Why don't you do something?' And inwardly screaming it at myself too.

My mother and I were at a stalemate. I persisted with the belief that if I would only try harder I could improve her life. Yet I never tried harder. My relationship to her was a series of good intentions which I never carried out. I had absorbed her passivity. The passivity consisted of choked down anger and distress. I wanted to offer her more of myself, yet I removed myself to the other side of the world.

When I think about how her death was a relief I think that some part of me had accepted that things would never change. I would not suddenly find it in me to send her that burst of energy that would enable her to walk again. I wouldn't even get around to writing to her or calling her more often. I was inadequate and my inadequacy was an ugliness I carried with me everywhere. I was frozen into a sense of myself which was rooted in the countless conflicting emotions I felt about her.

So one part of me had acknowledged the hopelessness of the situation, while another part of me judged that acknowledgement very harshly. Right through my twenties I had the sense of being tainted because I had given up. I had failed to keep trying to change things – in myself and for my mother.

The relief I felt at her death was, of course, deeply ambivalent. Yet there it was, undoubtedly real.

That she died when she did has enabled me to at least try and change how I am in the world. In that sense I feel it's quite lucky for me that she died while I was relatively young, that I got my chance early in my life. Now it's not her death I have to worry over, but what went before it and continues from it.

A Hard Death

May Sarton

We have seen how dignity can be torn
From the naked or the newly-born
By a loud voice or an ungentle presence,
Harshness of haste or lack of reverence,
How the hospital nurse may casually unbind
The suffering body from the lucid mind.
The spirit enclosed in that fragile shell
Cannot defend itself, must endure all
And not only the dying, helpless in a bed
Ask for a little pillow for the head,
A sip of water, a cool hand to bless:
The living have their lonely agonies.
'Is there compassion?' a friend asked me.
'Does it exist in another country?'

The busy living have no time to see
The flowers, so silent and so alive,
That paling to lavender of the anemone,
That purpling of the rose no one can save,
Dying, but at each second so complete
A photograph would show no slightest change.

Only the human eye, imperfect but aware,
Knows that the flower arrested on the air
Is flying through space, doing a dance
Toward the swift falls of petals, all at once.

God's Grace, given freely, we do not deserve,
But we can choose at least to see its ghost
On every face. Oh, we can wish to serve
Each other gently as we live, though lost.
We cannot save, be saved, but we can stand
Before each presence with gentle heart and hand;
Here in this place, in this time without belief,
Keep the channels open to each other's grief,
Never accept a death or life as strange
To its essence, but at each second be aware
How God is moving always through each flower
From birth to death in a multiple gesture
Of abnegation; and when the petals fall
Say it is beautiful and good, say it is well.

I saw my mother die and now I know
The spirit cannot be defended. It must go
Naked even of love at the very end.
'Take the flowers away' (Oh, she had been their
friend!)
And we who ached could do nothing more.
She was detached and distant as a star.

Let us be gentle to each other this brief time
For we shall die in exile far from home,
Where even the flowers can no longer save.
Only the living can be healed by love.

Stuck in Time

Barbara James

Throughout the summer before it became clear that my mother was dying, I fought with her, tooth and nail, non-stop. In this I was encouraged by other members of the family who were also confused and angered by my mother's seemingly irrational, clearly unpleasant behaviour. The summer was hot; all the windows were open for anyone in the vicinity to experience our family trauma along with us. There were many classic scenes, including one where I said I would 'rather turn tricks in the street' than continue to live with her another month. It was shortly after this battle that I announced that I was getting married, a coincidence that my mother did not hesitate to point out. For the rest of the time until the 'happy day' she refused to speak to me, and demonstrated her disapproval of my course (or recourse) of action by loudly crunching cough drops throughout the ceremony.

When my mother finally collapsed and was given a diagnosis of multiple myeloma, a cancer similar to leukaemia, she expressed relief that she finally knew what it was, that she was not losing her mind, simply her life. At the time of her diagnosis, Carolyn James had just turned forty-seven.

She had five children – four girls and a boy – of whom I am the oldest. Carolyn Katz married my father Hugh in her native New Jersey, where he had joined her after a summer job building fire stations in the British Columbia forests. They had met at university in Nova Scotia where she had gone for some unknown reason (although my assumption in youth had always been that it was to have me). After thirteen years of raising us, a job my mother freely admitted was horrendous, she got a teaching degree and took up paid employment. She immediately became a happier person, no longer restricted in her interests to the care of a large – in height, width and number – crowd of Jameses. My later-life feminist analysis of the trial it must have been for her to spend year after year cooped up with all of us, dependent on my father for money and having to debate every dish-washing and bedroom-tidying session with us, makes me more understanding of her position. At the time, though, she seemed much less than satisfactory as a mother.

I had often considered her to be odd and quite unlike the mothers of any of the other children at school, as far as I could tell. She yelled and threw pots and pans around the kitchen when she was angry, she didn't seem to appreciate the fact the grandma lived *right downstairs*, with Daddy's oldest sister; she made us make our own lunches. When we complained, as we usually did, that 'it's not MY job' to tidy up or do other unpleasant chores, she said it wasn't hers either. This left us speechless at her rebellion – everyone else knew what a mother's job was – why didn't she? However, in certain ways these differences had their advantages. I took pride in being unusual – an American mother lent me an air of cosmopolitan sophistication in Nova Scotia. Not to mention the glory of an atheist father and a Jewish grandfather in a claustrophobically Roman Catholic school – I was smug about being practically a pagan by their standards.

In almost every aspect of her life, my mother was full of contradictions. Being so fortunately free of all inconsistency, I considered myself the perfect person to point out all her flaws. Because of this attitude, disagreements about household duties and other aspects of our lives, there was a fairly high level of dispute between my mother and me throughout the time we knew each other. I particularly resented what I perceived as a completely hypocritical demand on my mother's part that while living in her house I had to go to church every Sunday (*and* Holy Days of Obligation). I decided that I hated the Catholic Church when I was ten after a number of the nuns' stories (such as the one where if you swing a set of rosary beads this act of disrespect will turn them into a snake) were proved – easily – false. I accused her of having a crush on Father McPherson, a youngish priest of the guitar mass school, which she didn't deny. After he left for a mission in Peru, a parish report that the priests were using the collection money for wall-to-wall carpeting and colour televisions brought an end to my mother's contributions. Although she never engaged in the cliquish church activities of many of the women in the area, she insisted upon attendance at Mass, resulting in an eleven-year battle between us. Eventually this was resolved simply by my being out of the house when it was known that a service was being held.

Fights about religion were far worse than discussions about sex, which simply didn't happen. We did not ever talk about sex, and barely breezed over periods (a mysterious Kotex booklet on menstruation – 'you **can** wear flowers, they will **not** wilt' – covered that topic). However, she often said that 'anyone who uses anything other than tampax is crazy,' a remark that would have caused toxic shock in most of the other mothers in my class, protective of their daughters' virginity. My mother's aphorisms were not the clean underwear reminders or other typical homey expressions of remembered youth. Her favourite was 'Chauvinism is something akin to insularity,' primarily loved for its euphonius nature. Her aspirations for us children were indirectly stated but very clear – to be well educated, witty, meeting our potential whatever it was and to behave above the common rabble. Although my definition of the common rabble is probably now the opposite of my mother's, and I am not successful in all my efforts, my aspirations are still the same as hers.

One time when her hospital bed was being lowered, my mother closed her eyes and crossed her arms over her chest with a flower from her bedside in her hands. Many people, especially those who don't know my sense of humour, find this unacceptably ghoulish, but it was not at all unusual for people in my family to react this way to death. The horror and sadness of death is not denied, but its humour is also accepted as natural – acknowledgement rather than denial. No one speaks in the standard euphemisms of death – no one 'passes away', 'goes to sleep' or 'is no more', they simply die. Death is not romanticised; neither is the dead person. No one kept my mother's ashes, although before she knew she was dying, she often expressed interest in being scattered 'from Yarmouth around to Liscombe' which was one of the weather pattern areas described on the daily forecast, another turn of phrase that appealed to her. I myself would like to be sprinkled on icy sidewalks, with the epitaph 'Useful Past the End'.

It has been suggested to me that I have a classic case of denial in my lack of active regret that my mother died, that without the benefit of therapy I have insufficient insight to be aware of my need for my mother and of my feelings about this loss. However, I had an intense eight-month period during which to think about little else than these points, with a few additional topics such as the meaninglessness of material possession. The eight months while she deteriorated were crystallised hell. As a family we seemed to accept quickly the fact that she was dying and to realise that any extra days or months were unexpected bonuses. Although I, too, immediately believed that she would not live long, watching the process of my mother's dying was endlessly terrible and lonely. I was unbearable to live with. I reacted by sleeping about eighteen hours a day, my waking hours spent sobbing or deep in thought. The worst moment came when I telephoned my mother and she told me through a haze of drugs that she was beginning to go blind because of the blood vessels breaking in her eyes. I ran to a friend's house crying for support, but she was unable to talk about it and changed the subject. I understand now that for many people such a plea for help is too overwhelming and that they simply feel inadequate, but at the time I felt only bitter and alone. When soon after this my mother told me that she didn't want to live any longer, that she felt as if she was being kept alive only to watch television, I was able to accept it, with much pain, and not beg her to fight on.

The surreal monotone of this whole time was epitomised by a bizarre incident. I spent the whole winter in a depressed state, almost in a trance. I was doing a degree in library science – what could seem more irrelevant? I had spent most of the morning at home, unable to do anything productive such as go to class or even read, my usually successful escape. The day was completely grey, from the low heavy sky to the solid, sharp, old snow and ice that clung to the ground, leaving uneven streaks of bare pavement. The air was bitterly cold: the hairs in my nose began to freeze. I walked along the street with little thought to my route: in my state of depressed oblivion it had become automatic. At the end of the block I saw a huge Husky lying in its yard, gnawing at something. I stopped to look at the dog. Its eyes were both a clear intense colour, but one was ice blue, the other gold. It paused to look at me, its paw holding down its meal. We stared at each other until the Husky remembered its main interest and continued to struggle with what it held in its paws. At that point I realised it was a kitten, half-consumed, long dead. I staggered away from this gory scene, unable to think. A bus with the destination marked 'Nowhere' drove past. I continued to school, dazed, with a feeling that I was completely removed from the reality of normal life. These strange-but-true visions seemed to fit with ease into the nightmare I was experiencing.

While my mother was alive, very little tenderness was expressed in my family. The most explicitly loving thing I can remember her saying was that the reason she liked me was because I had never told her I didn't believe in Santa Claus. I don't hold this general lack of spelled-out affection against her; neither do I hold her responsible for the dearth of hugs. This attitude came from both my parents' families and is still rampant in most of my relatives. But everyone felt loved, respected and included. Now that my mother has died, my father has married another woman who has encouraged him to express his feelings. He and I have even gone so far as to say that we love each other, an unheard-of statement in my childhood.

I am pretty certain that my mother would not approve of my life now. I suspect she would have stopped talking to me after John and I separated (not that she had wanted me to get married in the first place), let alone for my immediate reason for doing so – a change in sexual orientation. I know she would have been thrilled by my living in England, which she regarded as a quaint and bizarre but hilarious country based on our analysis of Monty Python (which we watched together every week), a thorough reading of ancient issues of *Country Life* and selected films such as the *St Trinian's* series. She would have loved my cooking but hated much of my politics. It is strange to speculate without a possibility of certainty. My relationship with her is stuck in time, and because of that I cannot imagine what changes might have taken place in her, as I have changed in the fifteen years since she died. It is possible that we might have grown closer and changed in some of the same directions. It is just as possible that we would have gone on to even more spectacular disagreements. In any case, my memory of her is one of mixed affection, irritation and love.

The night my mother was dying, the hospital, my siblings and I sat and watched a television programme about a woman who was unable to control her laughter at the funeral of an acquaintance, a television clown. We knew my mother would die soon; our father was at the hospital with her. She did not want to see us, she was drugged and bleeding everywhere. So we sat frozen in our seats, watching this ghoulishly appropriate comedy. I thought of this at my mother's funeral a couple of days later when Monsignor Murphy (he who benefited from the parish takings) mispronounced my mother's name as Caroline throughout the event. It is to my everlasting regret that I did not jump up and correct him. I didn't even have the nerve or energy to crunch coughdrops.

Most of the women in my family die young. Two of my aunts died of breast cancer. My brother, a multi-media artist, died four years ago at the age of twenty-nine, not long after his musical hit 'Gum Disease' made the Nova Scotia chart. I have experienced long, slow death up close, and sudden, unexpected death from afar. Too many people have died already. I am inured not to death itself, but to its presence. Although I do not dwell on the deaths of these many close people, they have profoundly affected me. For one thing I am practically counting on not having to worry about a pension.

I suppose the major effect on me of my mother, brother, aunts and grandparents dying is that I have become more of a realist, or what many call a pessimist. It's not that I expect all my friends and relatives to die, but I don't expect them never to die, and I never make promises that I'll be around in thirty years (though I am willing to plan trips far enough in advance to get discount flights). I am also pretty neurotic in my reaction to phone calls at odd hours, since the announcement of my brother's death was by telephone. All my sisters know to begin a long-distance conversation with reassurances that all is well.

One good result of all this death is that I try – with varying degrees of success – to work out disagreements with people I care about and not let them brew. I am happy that I remember my mother as I felt towards her when she was alive: neither sanctified nor vilified in death, but strong, stubborn, caring, wild and funny – all I could ask for in my mother.

Yellow Topping:
Martha Joy Marr

Emma Hindley

Damaged people are dangerous. They carve a steep path through your life, and then they leave. Just like that. Without a word. Or none that you were told.

As a child you have no power to demand an answer or an explanation, especially when the leaving is painful (or shameful even).

My mum was beamed up by Scottie and I don't remember the last time I saw her.

I try to remember a look or a hug, some good time, alone together. Going shopping down the Holloway Road, letting me bunk off school, she bought floating candles and we ate by candle-light in the power cuts of 1972.

There's little else – my memory is like some old bed-wetting stain: it fades over the years.

Little me, sat on a yellow candlewick bedspread, rivulets of pattern picked out in soft, brushed up waves. Pale baby yellow. My dad's huge hands – pulling at me – crying like a big kid – and I knew this was it, before he'd even said a word. I knew this was the moment: I wasn't a whole child anymore but a motherless child and so only partial.

I have some memories of her that are mine. I have lots

from other people: of the erratic, exciting, unusual mother of four that was her self-made image. The one that I was really proud of as she picked me up from school in her trendy Afghan coat.

My strongest memories are the ones I pretended I didn't have, of snide comments and depressed, speechless Saturday afternoons. I made pots of tea to try and cheer her up.

I used to measure my life in terms of how long I have gone without her: it's a year since she died, it's five years, and now it's eighteen, part of me is still behaving like that eleven-year-old. At least I have given up feeling guilty when I resent other people's mothers. Feeling jealous when they go shopping together or chat about the intimate details of their lives. I even feel jealous of friends who don't get on with their mothers: it brings out all the worst of the 'at least you've got one' in me. It's not exactly a grown-up way to feel, and the eleven-year-old that lurks inside me comes out when I least expect her – 'I want/it's not fair.' I'm nearly thirty and sometimes I cry like a baby. Do people ever get over these things? Will I?

My mother drifts across the years to me, in isolated, often ordinary moments but more often in confusing feelings of helplessness: a depressing sense of not really knowing what is going on. Knowledge is not only power to a child, but more clearly it can dispel fear and confusion...

I look at children of the same age as I was and wonder how it was I had no idea – how excitedly I ran up the stairs to the room with that yellow candlewick bedspread and the holiday-let curtains. It had to be something exciting because Daddy wanted to talk to me on my own. And what was the matter with everyone? – they all seemed so miserable and teary – and we were meant to be on holiday as well. And now, how easily I avoid what's going on, how easily I can pretend that there's nothing wrong, '*I'm* not upset,' and that everyone will believe me.

I look at myself now and wonder: is my body like hers was? Would her clothes have fitted me? Her rings do – I treasure them with a stubborn possessiveness.

I cannot ask him. It is still too sore – we still behave towards each other like that yellow candlewick day. I cannot cause him more pain. We're too awkward and yet I cling to him like that child. Why is she so rarely mentioned?

I feel jealous of my brothers and sister, of the age they were, of those who knew her this much, and who were this close to her – who knew her at all. And then there's me, who knew nothing. I often say this but it's not just a lack of memory. The memories I do have I remember as a child would, a day, a moment or an event: not a whole person. How much is really my own recollection? Often it's things I've been told and so I worry myself by thinking they're not really mine.

I feel angry – not with her of course, not yet – but with friends, who talk about period pains, relationships, clothes, jobs, the price of bread, with such assumption. I'm angry because of things I don't have – a hug of sympathy ('Never mind, love, you're better off without her'), of congratulations ('I'm so proud of you sweetheart'), of support ('So she's left you – she wasn't worth it') knowing that not all of my friends have these wonderful, perfect relationships with their mothers (but at least they've got them...).

Angry for how it made me feel, and still does, for all those people who crossed the road in embarrassment, of not knowing what to say, for my terror of the inevitable question 'How?' I used to lie and say she'd died of cancer and then feel awful. I always felt ashamed and cheated somehow – no innocent, unavoidable end – fighting for life against disease – no tragic death under a speeding car – no tear-stained final farewell. I still feel terrible for even thinking these things. And now, when people ask, I receive their embarrassment with such natural acceptance. After all, I've had time to get used to it. Will I always carry this shame? However much I attempt to excuse her awful act by her awful life, her unstable state of mind, there is the child that cries 'How could you do this if you really loved us?'

When I started secondary school some six months later, I felt like the whole school knew about my loony mum topping herself. I would studiously avoid any discussion of parents and thankfully my dad was talked about as good-looking, so that distracted them from mothers and let me off the hook. My first gym lesson, rows of eleven-year-olds in gym-kits, all with neatly embroidered initials in bright red, except mine... the teacher called me up to have a go: 'Why hasn't your mother sewed your initials on?' Silence. 'Oh yes... well can't *you* do it?' This was to be the first of many classroom skirmishes concerning sick notes, lunch money or complaints: the teachers were always forgetting, even though I knew they had all been told. Whenever I got into trouble I'd get those sympathy-ridden, patronising looks from them. It was the best excuse yet. Later, my slightly unusual home and my lovely, spoil-you-rotten dad were seen as a great asset by friends. There was even talk that I lived in a commune – they said we all smoked dope and had a wild time, which did my image no end of good except I still felt like a freak... 'and, well, you know about her mum... '

On holiday with family and friends, my dad had stayed in London – I don't remember questioning why – I don't even remember my mum disappearing. He arrived surrounded by weeping people, took me upstairs and sat me on the bed. I could see his big veiny hands, shaking. I ran my finger down a ridge of fluffy yellow candlewick – casually – I remember wondering what was going on.

My dad's words stumbled out over tears, so weak, so frightened and so frightening in his weakness. 'Dead' is a hard word to understand immediately. She'd driven her van to Mornington Crescent, wrapped herself up in a blanket, taken all her Mandrax and died alone, her shopping basket by her side. This image is perfectly formed and held in my mind: I must have asked for every last detail, as it never completely leaves me.

Clinically planned and carried out – as people who are desperate to die often behave – I still don't know if she left a note. I do know now just how desperately she didn't want to live anymore. I had not been told about previous attempts: of my father stopping her, my brothers finding her and then she simply disappeared – and still I wonder at my playful candlewick innocence.

And so now I'm a grown-up, I look secretively for my mother – as if it's something to be embarrassed about. I don't ask but I wonder: do I look like her in any way, do I behave like her? I ask my dad but he is very diplomatic and says we all do.

I went to Scotland – to find the places that she ran from – to my romantic idea of a loch-side town, only to find a shit-heap full of Orangemen and rubbish. Then on to Glasgow, to the house I can remember her talking about, to find it had been knocked down, years ago. Finally to the loch I've dreamt of (her last resting place I heard only recently), to find an American Naval Base, full of swarthy Yanks in base-ball caps. I think I've finally made my peace with Scotland.

I wonder why you catch up on me every five years or so, Mother – will I ever be rid of you? I used to pretend it had done me some good – toughened me up, made me different – then my big relationship ended and I went through the same old shit.

When I started to fall in love with women, a tortured adolescent if ever there was one, it felt like another curse, sent from her grave. A connection only I could suggest: anybody else tried it and I'd smack their face in. That made me even more of a misfit, and a pervert to boot, but more so, a fact I derived some morbid satisfaction from because I felt I had no control over it; 'I fancy girls, right? I can't help it if I don't fancy boys.' When I fell helplessly in love with yet another girl at school, I agonised over the idea that everyone knew I was only queer because my nutty mother had topped herself.

So, do I look for my mother in the arms of other women? Do I really give a shit?

I found someone I could celebrate Mother's Day with; we gave each other presents in their absence, joking about it with friends who'd been for real Mother's Day lunches with live mothers and bunches of flowers. I felt embarrassed about it, as if we were making such a fuss about a sick joke. You weren't, you were arrogant, 'It's their problem with dead mothers,' you said. Why am I so disgraced by all of this still? I make jokes about not being able to iron or cook (both of which I do passably well). No maternal influence you see. I think my mothered friends are getting bored with all of this.

Sitting in the kitchen, I would find him late at night, red-eyed and soggy, crying quietly in a corner over letters of condolence. Or at breakfast time when the post had just arrived. Luckily my dad has always been good at crying, but it did worry me: what if he got so miserable that... ?

My big strong dad, with those big veiny hands, the man who could explain nothing to me, crying. I remember worrying that he'd start crying in the street, in front of all those snotty people who'd look sympathetically at us but could never quite bring themselves to say anything. We'd hold hands so tight, watching people we knew whispering ('so sad, what a brave man') as they crossed the road to avoid us, or shut their doors. Like the memorial service in our local church, everybody was there, everybody knew, it was full of neighbours, crying dramatically. I stood at the front, in my best dress which I hated. All I can remember is our family standing in the front row, me being very brave, not crying. I couldn't, not in front of all those people. Until the last moment: I burst, I couldn't help it, it was all so confusing.

He would never talk about her (and rarely does now) but would gorge himself on condolences, read and reread them, as if he was punishing himself for his imagined guilt in it all. On days when I was off school and alone in the house, I would sneak into his study and pull out the battered old plastic bag that held the letters. I read them guiltily and feverishly, mortified at the front-page article from our local paper ('Local doctor's wife takes own life') which he had cut out.

At times I so desperately wanted her with me, and still do if I dare be so terrifyingly honest. I remember being on holiday the year after the event and praying grievously to some god to send her ghost, just for a chat or a cuddle, if nothing else.

My mum could have been a designer (she was good at art), an Olympic hurdle champion (she won medals at school), a world-class model (she was pretty), a nurse (which she trained as), a book critic (she devoured them) or an insomniac expert (she devoured Mandrax just as easily). I could have had a wonderful, honest, loving relationship with her (but I doubt it somehow) or a terrible, tempestuous, trauma-filled time (more likely). All of these fantasies I can indulge in endlessly because they are unanswerable. My mum and me are like a blank sheet of paper: I can fill it in whichever way I want, except of course it's not a very satisfying activity. I rarely dream of her – she is buried far too deep in me for that – so I make up stories to myself instead.

What a cow, leaving us all like that. Crazy fucking loony woman; sad, depressing, sick, creepy nutter. You can't always be the blameless, innocent victim mother: you have made one out of me for far too long. How dare you die this romantic, confusing death when it's really all about drama and cowardice? I've heard the stories, of the beautiful, energetic, charismatic woman whose terrible mysterious early life was just too tragic to bear. I know them to be true, but anger is healthy, I think, and the best balance to pain.

The cremation. I remember the burning – crammed into my sister's car, in my favourite outfit. Sat on my brother's knee. Engulfed in a silence we could not begin to fill, he squeezed me so tight I could hardly breathe. I'd stopped thinking days before and was just existing, not even reacting. When we arrived at the crematorium I felt exposed and pitied, not sad but on display. I even felt embarrassed at the piles and piles of flowers.

The vicar had finished her 'favourite' poems (how do you choose poems for someone who wanted to die?) and reached the 'ashes to ashes' bit. When the doors opened mechanically and the coffin glided away from me, I panicked: had anyone remembered to take her glasses off? What was she wearing? A long white thing? Did she look as beautiful dead? Why couldn't I see her? Why hadn't she wanted to see me before she did it? Why couldn't I see her? I still hold the picture in my head, and luckily it's beautiful and peaceful.

Afterwards, we all went for a meal at a local steakhouse. This was alternately uncomfortably silent or desperately chatty. My godmother, whom I hadn't seen for years, gave me a little flowery jug and bowl. It was sweet of her but I remember thinking at the time, what is this all about?

Dreams of my Mother comfort me

Caroline Halliday

Tonight the sculpture on the South Bank is a brilliant cypher. One stationary bar of dark blue, two diagonals of acid yellow, and below at an angle, red, with one distant line of green. Outlined against dark sky it looks like distant ships against a black sea.

In the time it takes me to look down and up again it has changed. Purple flickers and flashes from side to side, multitudes of purple neon light, like a child jumping from one leg to the other, very fast. The diagonals of the skipping legs as well as the verticals. The purple, perhaps it is lilac/mauve, is everywhere, moving so fast. There is yellow light too. But one bar of green stays motionless, and one of yellow. Fixed points in a sea of motion.

Then back to something statuesque. The dark blues are poised at the head of the outline. Steady and remote. With green and yellow diagonal, and at the bottom two red lines flash, like codes, like the tip of an artist's brush, or the tip of a tongue. Very minimalist. Very delicate.

Comfort: to strengthen: relieve from pain or distress: soothe, cheer.

*My mother is sitting beside me on my old settee, the sur-
face of it rough. We are looking at a book together. Sharing
something. When I realise/remember that she can't be
there because she's dead, I turn towards her. Wanting her to
be there. Please. I turn and put my hand on her leg. And as
I do so, she disappears. She's not there.*

   *Yet it is something to know that she was there, just for
that short moment.*

From the time my friend Mandy began to talk about her
approaching death to the day she died, could have been four
years. In the last year she talked clearly about it. I talked
with her. So did others. I made a serious effort to be there,
to recognise it, to be as honest as I could. I'd been close to
death in my work, a woman who'd died of cancer, a baby's
cot death. *But I knew nothing.*

Mandy died in October. Two months later my father died
suddenly on 26th December, the day after Christmas, and
then eight months after him, my mother died.

   I wasn't prepared. I knew nothing.

Because I knew nothing, because these deaths gave me both
frightening grief, but also at times something like wonder,
and a knowledge I never had before, I want to write not
about the grieving, the terror of it, but about some of the
privilege I feel to have known these people's deaths and
some of the few things that have meant comfort. It was a
time of little comfort.

   I want to write this with the sun on my face. The sun
comforts me: I feel it again. Once I wondered if I would ever
feel simple things like that, in the same way. Now I can lie
back on park benches, with the sun on my face.

When I returned to London from my mother's funeral it was to an empty house, my daughter away. Several people knew my mother had died. No one offered anything and I didn't know what to ask for. After I'd asked once or twice for various things I gave up asking. I expected I should 'get back to normal now'. It was such a powerful expectation. And I failed, over and over again I failed, until I had to recognise my life had broken down. I couldn't carry on.

Comfort: pen and large sketch pad. Draw anything. Sit on the floor in the corner of the room, like a child banished to the corner for being naughty. Cry and draw, draw and cry. There is nothing else to do.

What I wanted, have always wanted, was someone to hold me till I stopped crying. Someone who would put up with shouting and screaming, hitting and banging until I fell down exhausted. What I did in that first week was to draw and to speak to my therapist. Every day.

I had to hold things together. Not collapse. What I wanted most of all was to give up.

In those first couple of days after my mother died I wanted rituals, sackcloth and ashes. I wanted to smear dirt on my head, and wanted to rend my clothes. I found some china that belonged to her and alone I smashed it. I found some of her old clothes and I tore them.

I had constantly the desire/the image of leaping into her grave, the only image that made sense.

the place to register this:
cauldron of earth
veins of a tree
hammering iron
tearing at sand

the place to register:
muscle pushing
scream of child
pulling down a cloud
stopping the wind

Leaping into my mother's grave   necessary madness   I think that for a long time I have been mad. At least this is the only way I can describe the grieving, my collapse. Madness makes more sense than grief.

The days before her funeral were ones of shock and terror. Terror that I alone had these feelings. No one, no one at all shared them.

I put some wildflowers in my mother's hands in her coffin. On her coffin, as it was lowered into the grave, I placed white flowers of Russian vine, *Poliganum ballsquanicum*, the only Latin plant name I know. My eldest sister and I gathered them by the canal in Oxford. It was something my mother had planted over the fence outside her kitchen in our first house. Something she saw daily when I was a child. It was a family joke, this long Latin name that all of us could reel off.

On her coffin, never mind what the watching people thought, I put a single rose, and dead leaves which fluttered as she was lowered into the hole in the red earth, the ground, which is what we do with people who are dead. The leaves fluttered in the current of air as she was moved, leaves dead but moving, like the fluorescent life of the neon South Bank sculpture.

These were the rituals I was allowed, these were the rituals others could bear that I could perform in front of them, or behind their backs.

The last time I saw my mother,
she was dead. Her face falling,

over the time allowed, into separateness.
I say I won't be squeezed into your timetable.
Find the place to stop, then ask me again.

Heartbeats. You say you need to understand
death in life. Not your hands to hold mine.
That would pierce the screaming
or at least, begin. Too long.
I need to find my mother, in death,
in that child struggling to stand.

Ritual: Bracken, paths through trees, hillside, the gesture of throwing   letting something go   stones, small stones   trying to let something go
  large pine trees touch each trunk feel their strength count the years of my mother's life   trees   strength mothers   my mother   I lie with my back on the bracken and ferns in the woods and look up at the tree above me.

Most of Mandy's funeral was arranged by her before she died, but as we arrive at the crematorium   pallbearers   large men clad in black coats   I didn't want them to carry Mandy between rows of women her mother lesbians friends men   I wanted us to do it to take her to her last physical place   'I would like us to carry her' I said to the woman funeral director   I walked along rows of women waiting outside the chapel asking her closest friends if they would like to carry Mandy
  six of us   roughly equal shoulder height we step backwards from the hearse to instructions Mandy in her coffin is rolled onto our shoulders
  Mandy my head beside her she lies by my right ear this is the last of her   this is her final place after this anything

physical of her will be gone
  this is so strange so incomprehensible

  Comfort: we carried you.

Mandy gave me so many gifts in relation to her death. It was
a gift to be able to talk to her about it. It was a gift to know
her and know what she was able to accept about death. It
was a gift from her of the experience of her death itself. She
gave me the courage to know that whatever happened it was
still her, still Mandy lying there, still Mandy going to be cremated. Not the body, not the deceased, but Mandy, still
Mandy. Still Mandy only now just her body, her body with
animation disappeared.

Gifts I carried on to my parents' deaths.

And then, the last few days I spent with my mother, looking after her. Early mornings. Cool air coming through the
open door to the garden. Me staggering with needing to
sleep, seven o'clock, eight o'clock. It was so tiring. The
emotional strain, all the patterns I wasn't used to, that
weren't mine.

  If we could have been alone more, just her and me. A
woman to care for me, and me to care for her.
Companionable it was.

  Throughout my life, my mother gave the impression she
would always be there. She was rarely ill. She never went
away. She was never in hospital. Her life was grafted onto
her family. Her message was – I am eternally your mother.
Mothers are always there –

  All this despite the fact that she hadn't been there. She

hadn't protected me from my father, she hadn't protected me from the pain of being a woman, from her own and the world's rejection of my falling in love with a young woman. My father always came first. She modified what he did and said, but never stopped him completely. This is the nature of a woman's life under patriarchy. This was the nature of the life of the woman who died.

After my father died, my mother lived for eight months. It was the first and perhaps the only time I saw her, her alone, in command of her life. Perhaps it was the first time in her life.

She had made us reorganise the bedroom very quickly. To a single person's room. The change was dramatic: the double bed no longer dominated the room. It was her bedsit now, the room from which she managed the last of her world, and the last of her life. She was easy on big things, emphatic on the small things that made her life bearable. I think she stayed alive to see us through.

And I wasn't there when she died. Both my sisters were there.

The lesbian who had emphasised I had to support my own family: my own life. I was away on a course, so I wasn't disturbed. The independent lesbian...isn't called till too late. Yes, I am bitter. Being with my mother as she died would have helped me to accept her death, feel that I said goodbye. It was an honour I didn't receive.

A house with all my family, my parents, my two sisters. Filthy house. No one cares. I am furiously distressed and no one takes any notice. I go into a large empty room, filthy. My sister follows me around trying to say it isn't true that no one notices. I howl and scream, devastated. The feelings

*I couldn't express in daytime. She'll give up I know. I want
my mother to hold me. I cry and cry. She comes forward. I
put my arms round her and cry and scream.*

It is good that she holds me.

I wake, I am crying and crying.
*I am not even in the house with them. My mother is not
even alive.*

The day of my mother's funeral   flowers   three big bunches sent from my daughter   from her other mother   they
were all in France   there were large red gerbera among them
then more flowers   more more   My sister and I finding
vases from all around the house   borrowing vases the work
made my back ache I was exhausted   never surrounded by
so many flowers they were everywhere   red and pink   white
and orange   purple and yellow   beautiful and fragrant they
owed nobody anything   they waited for nothing they asked
for nothing they were just there being themselves   colourful   scented   fragile
    there were flowers on the kitchen table   on the floor   on
the kitchen surfaces   flowers among my mother's kitchen
things   the wooden spoons   the thing you use for mashing
potatoes   flowers in my mother's own vases   that had
names – the large blue one   the white one I got as a wedding
present   the one with the stripes round oh yes I don't like
that one so much – vases she liked and treasured and held
and caressed and arranged flowers in this kitchen table with
its green formica top   that she worked at and wiped and
moved around in her kitchen but she hadn't worked in the
kitchen for ages   she was too weak   instead it was the place
I mixed the Complan taking wicked spoonfuls of the thick
sweet gooey mixture   the too sweet necessity to spoon it

into my mouth   my child's mouth   my baby mouth   wanting something thick and gooey and me the baby needing baby food so that I could feed my mother help my mother eat

but here was her kitchen   the green formica top   and we spread and chose and arranged   beautiful fragile blossoms choosing and placing and looking   we lost ourselves among the flowers   while all the while she was lying there dead while all the while she lay there dead   and we touched flowers   we held and cut and ached and chose and moved   never so many flowers in my whole life   getting lost inside this have I told you how it was the way of knowledge of life's strangeness   have I told you

I dreamt I went into hospital to see Mandy. It was strange to dream about her in a hospital because she would never have allowed herself to go into hospital and I was under a vow never to let her go in either.

She was sitting up in bed wearing something bright turquoise, and she was not ready to be seen, but as I went through the door she turned to me, and welcomed me with her own dear scratchy voice, cracking away, 'Caroline... ' and I took her in my arms.

In these dreams, she fades gradually in my arms into nothing.

The night Mandy died, she came to visit me. I knew she was there, in my kitchen, just up by the dining-room table, a place she's sat in the wheelchair to eat. And there she was in the wheelchair. The image was fleeting.

I want her here now, in my living room.

I want you back again, and you'll never be back again. *Never* is such a long word. Never is such a mortal word. Never means that I will die too. Never means that things

pass and they don't return. And we change, getting irrevo-
cably closer to our own deaths. Such a little time.

*I dream the phone rings and when I answer it, it is Mandy's
voice just as usual. 'Hello, Caroline, it's Mandy. How are
you?' – these phone dreams are so powerful, the person's
voice exact, the experience so much a reality – it is wonderful to hear her voice, and I begin to talk to her.*

*Then she says 'Do you want to hear about the place I'm
in?' I begin to listen and then something happens. I remember with some part of my brain that Mandy is dead and it
is impossible (I think) for me to hear about the place she's
in. My brain jams, like radio interference, loud, frightening.*

*And this is the same dream... I am in my bedroom with
my sister, and Mandy is asleep in the bed. The window is
slightly open and a breeze blows the curtain, I am afraid of
what is outside the window. Mandy is asleep in the bed
and I reach out my hand to touch her forehead, her broad,
pale forehead with freckles, that is so dear and familiar,
and as soon as I touch her my hand fuses to her forehead
and she is dead and I am terrified, my hand fused to her. I
turn to speak to my sister, but my voice won't come, I
struggle to whisper   force my voice out*

It was so sad this dream, because it was so terrifying. I had
no fear of Mandy, alive or dead, but in the dream the images
of dead people, of the horror of them, of ghoulish things and
fear, all these images forced on us, rose up in me despite my
total rejection of them.

*One of the few measures of defiance from my mother
this worn cap, a man's, my father's,
torn, worn in bed in the hospital
a defence against unwanted light*

shielding her eyes.
she looked as she never did before,
cheeky, boyish, defiant

the other time in Norfolk
long sandy beaches 1950s empty
and us, the family, three girls and a husband,
long sandy beaches, empty, and us with no costumes.
my mother suddenly says Yes, I'll do it
strips off all her clothes
in front of shocked daughters
and heads for the sea

my mother died on August third   August third to February third is half a year   half a year since my mother's death   the two days are like an eyelet lining up with another   the clear sight right through two eyeholes. Metal clean rounded two needles' eyes. It is harder for us to go through the eye of a needle than...

February third, I knew the day had clarity   clean through a single clear note a bell across country sounding across half a year

the two dates balancing somewhere and with me is her face her breath her smile ready leaning forward half apologetic, anticipatory

that blouse   she wore those trousers, trying to keep warm, of softness of them   that warm, thick grey   these textures

the tassels of her mother's rug, parted by her fingers, like a child convalescing, stroking and parting the tassels...

I am in a large building, a school, with both my parents

and others. A tidal wave is coming. I can see it in the distance. The water will rush through the building, trap us all as it surges up to the ceilings. We have to go further and further back through the building, to escape it. I am encouraging everyone to move.

My mother refuses to go. I struggle on, away, though I have to leave her. Eventually, I reach the back of the building, climb railings, get to higher ground. I know that she will die, but that she is dead already.

Drowning. It reminded me of being under the waves at Black River, Mauritius, down down down, boiling water and grit and sand and water pushing me down. Floating clear eventually, but would there have been any air, any space that wasn't water, if this tidal wave swept through the buildings? and my mother would have drowned, but then she's dead already –

the year as it changes is a wheel turning a circle, with symbolic section July my birthday is at the bottom of the wheel New Year balances at the top and then the year curves round to Easter

April spring what it meant for me was that the year was no longer travelling away from my mother's death, but towards it. Instead of time taking me away, the year was swinging round to come closer. I was coming back closer to the time she died.

April was terrifying

whatever I had not faced whatever I had not dealt with I knew I would have to face as the year came round whatever I thought time would help to heal became as exposed as it ever had been there was no way to escape it

I faced this other this second period of collapse of grief madness alone as before searching always searching who understands where are people what am I doing wrong why

am I so alone
    I was returning to Leicester   the place I was in when my
mother died it terrified me
    another long period of grief   madness

I write this with a sense of the madness and its aloneness
with a sense of writing for others who are alone who feel the
madness of their feelings which others don't want to hear

*We are all playing in a stream, my mother is there, we are
playing with wooden ducks that float and then her duck
goes right under the bridge and we chase it, we must get it
back, we follow the course of the stream and chase it, up
this steep rocky dangerous place, nearly falling, while it
sails off down the river*
    *We go round another way, into the town – shops and so
on – and the river down the middle of the street, and ask
people 'Have you seen the wooden duck?'*
    *Then I decide we're in the wrong place, and go back
downstream and the stream has dried up, it is very grassy...*
    *But of course finding this duck for my mother is a sym-
bol of finding her life for her... and I know I should have
stayed right by her, not gone off on this task... not left her...*

    Ritual: I take a stone from every place I visit. I take
    some earth from every place I visit. I leave behind some
    earth from my garden, and a stone.

    The places I visit do not bring comfort without pain. I will
never walk footpaths with my father again.
    But it is to honour these places, my experience. In these
places I honour myself.

    Comfort: writing.

Comfort: a rug I have bought in Derbyshire. Jacobs
wool. Thick, soft, grey, white, brown.

It has proved incredibly hard to make this writing work. I
don't usually have such repeated difficulty. It refuses to set-
tle into a style that feels OK. I write notes to myself: 'get rid
of the short sentences, don't write in the present tense, too
stilted, write in a different style' and I change some of it and
it improves and then it foils my attempts again and feels
uncomfortable, wrong. I know when my writing is working
and this isn't.

I give up entirely. I cannot write about death, I cannot be
a writer and write about death.

I am depressed, confused, frightened, writing has always
brought me comfort and this won't.

I cannot write about death without reminding myself
what is life, why I am alive. So I give up and go for walks in
the park.

I remind myself it is all only for me, and that doesn't
work. I wouldn't be typing and changing, typing and changing if it was only for me, it would all rest as it does in the
corners of my body, in the private occasions, the evenings,
the night-times when I can't pretend any more, although I
am 'back to normal' now, when I cannot pretend it doesn't
hurt, that it has gone or been dealt with. It is less frightening but not gone. It would all rest in notebooks, the black
and red Chinese notebooks, which I wish to burn soon, burn
before I die so that no one no one has to hold them, store
them, read them, think about the pain in them.

It is impossible to make 'art', make something deliberately
something beautiful about this question of death.

    becoming an artist, making it into 'writing', cuts me off
from the pain, separates me from what I feel about my

mother's death. Makes me the writer 'creating'... I can't bear it.

> *if she lies there*
> *too small to reckon with earth*
> *slashed sides red earth*
> *if she lies there*
> *too small for the weight of it*
> *flowers under the storms of rain*
> *dead flowers   purple and blue*
>
> *and a cat watches*
> *watching me in the back garden*
> *meeting me eye on eye*
> *why should I want*
> *to tear at grass stems*
>
> *why is the word unbearable*
> *so empty*
> *so proper on the phone*
> *tell me a language*
> *tell me a word to use*
>
> *tell me sound*
> *apart from screaming*
>
> *tell me how heavy grass sounds*
> *how unbearable*

I didn't want to stay at the family house when I went back on the anniversary of my mother's death. I still felt the way I always had, submerged by my family, its notions which hung on over me, me the lesbian, the different one, no matter how much I asserted myself, no matter that my family 'accepted' who I was. I didn't want to stay there. But I knew if I didn't it would hurt my sister, she would not be able to understand this rejection.

It was hot. So hot. I didn't want to be in the house. And suddenly it occurred to me that I could sleep in the summer house.

Night-time. Night air.

Sleeping there was the nearest I could be to my mother's bedroom. The place where she lay and looked at the garden. She sat up in bed with the TV on at all hours when she couldn't sleep.

This was where she was when she phoned me. This was one place I could imagine her.

Sleeping out there I could almost see her bedroom door. The night was full of the only element of her presence I have, air.

Comfort: Marigolds. My mother's flower.

Ritual: The last things I did with my mother were ordinary things, watching TV, buying bread and fish for our lunch. I drove her, or wheeled her, she suggested, directed, she was somehow frail but free, in charge, we were two free individuals, joined by nothing but what we did together. Except that we bought wrapping paper for a present, and cards and chocolates.

now it is a year later   now it is the same day   the same day and then the next day   I am in Oxford   I am visiting places making a network   a web of places making peace with places and memories putting things in their places stones earth   water   fire

and as I begin to drive away from Oxford wandering

through Summertown to the London Road   I am driving
small street   memory my mother says down here this is the
fish shop   and I go in   she is   I am her chauffeur   we drive
if we want to if she can manage it these last few days

these rare and rich and only days with my mother and no
one else do you understand my mother and no one else

me and this old woman   and I want to tear the paper right
across do you understand

a fish shop is it?
do you understand?

on my way back to London   it was going past the fish shop
made me cry   I parked the car, and walked down the street
visiting each shop we went in, when she was alive. I bought
bread, I bought retsina, my favourite drink. I bought chocolates and wrapping paper in the same shop I'd stood in with
my mother. I photographed the street.

I want my mother back so badly. I want to push her in the
wheelchair down this street and do these things that are so
easily seen as unimportant. Buying bread and carrots.

do you understand?

Ritual: when we were children our garden ended on the
banks of the River Wandle. I was a water child, always
in, on, exploring that river, the river of my childhood. it
was my safe place, my place of freedom. Rowing,
bathing, swimming, splashing.

I went to Wolvercote in Oxford. It was a hot, hot day.
I swam in the river water. Alone, surrounded by families, and heterosexual couples, and children. For me it
was a ritual. Water, river water. Recognition. This is,
this has been, this will always be.

Ritual: a weekend workshop on loss. Movement, music, sounds, an African myth of the woman and the mustard seed. I sat surrounded by women who sang, high, low, fast, slow, harmonising or not. Swimming in sound, resting in sound, held by sound, their voices. On the outside of the circle, I used my voice, finding notes that meant goodbye. Over and over, goodbye. Four notes.

Ritual: I visited my mother's grave, and I sang the same four notes.

It is all about Honour.

I want to walk with my mother around Oxford, with the wheelchair. Naming ourselves the centre of what we do, making ourselves important. Her and me. A woman in a wheelchair and her daughter. I want to be visible. I want to be present, concrete. I want to be seen by you. Think about it when you next see us. A woman, the mother and the daughter, the child. The woman who will die. The daughter who will grieve. Now they are together. Soon they will be apart. *Honour us.*

There is no comfort in this.

I simply want that time again.

For a lesbian, what is this bond with her mother? For me, my mother was the heterosexual woman who gave me life, who nurtured me badly or well. In the way she thought she should. She gave me too many images of 'the mother', and didn't acknowledge the lie this was. In this life, a heterosexual woman can only lie to a lesbian. It isn't a question of choice it is a question of allegiance. And hers was to him. Mine to create an allegiance to myself and other women.

Was I trying to change the bonding? From her to other women? Symbolically she will always be the woman who betrayed me.

But I have begun to accept that she was also the woman who loved me. And to me this is one of the contradictions I learn slowly to live with.

I want my mother back. I loved her. She loved me. No one will ever again love me like that.

When I was a child, aged five, I had a life-threatening illness: they thought I was going to die. My mother stayed with me all the time. She wanted me to live. I feel as though I have to relive that experience, as though I have to choose to live this time.

For the most part of these two years there were many times when I wanted to be dead. Wanted to die. Death was so much nearer to me. About life I felt hopeless.

There were three long periods in this last year, when I was so overwhelmed by all that had happened and was happening. It took me five months to feel able to cope with the basic necessities of my life: to look after myself and my daughter and be able to work and write again. In those five months I didn't do more than a few days' work outside my house. My life fell apart. The communication I felt able to make didn't work, I was constantly frightened of collapse and I think rightly knew that no one at all could have given me what I needed. No one.

And then again in April I was crazy again and in July as the day came closer   3rd August   but I went through it again with my sister's help I pre-lived it my fear of grief my fear of terror and I was ready when the day came

it had to be my way in the end how I spent the day   a beautiful hot summer's day meandering my way to Oxford, to Stanton St John a village my parents had lived at   at my

own pace and with stops and detours as I needed to take
them with stones candles water earth photos of my mother
notebook and my car my dear dear car

and so I come to the end of the writing – the end of the rituals the forms of comfort   and the dreams I want to write
about   not the end of dreams about my mother nor the end
of grieving

but the uncertain place
death sitting right in the middle of the living room
right here by the fire   with my pyjamas and dressing gown
with the fire too hot and the night too late
Finally finally the end   and the beginning of thinking   this
is working this does convey something   this is something
like what I had in mind
and it will be finished
and then I will start again maybe
with another piece of writing   with all the other things I
haven't said here   how she looked   who she was

> *I dream I am in my parents' house and they are out for
> the evening. They come home, through the front door,
> my mother in her red coat, and wearing her Sherlock
> Holmes hat with the ear flaps. She takes off her coat,
> they both go past me, and then I turn realising the
> strangeness of this, they are both dead, but have just
> come in, I walk through the room to look for my moth-
> er and she comes towards me, she holds out her hands
> to me, she looks me in the face. I look her in the face,
> for a long time, for the first time.*
>
> *I can't describe this dream properly   I can't express
> the meaning of it to you*
>
> *the movements I make from the telephone   my par-*

ents entering   out for the evening enjoying themselves
entering in outdoor clothes   her coat so familiar the
red twist of the wool, the tweed texture the kind of
check in the fabric   her hat under which her wisps of
hair   the hair I used to cut for her sometimes   the hair
so like mine   how my hair will be the texture of hers
they are happy   the times they might have come in
and I didn't greet them   not properly not knowing   oh
one day there will be a last time   and then   then it will
be over you don't think like this you don't know this
then   these people come in a house through their own
front door I am on the telephone I don't disregard them
but I am not overwhelmed with the pleasure of seeing
them we don't value people enough

   I turn they are in the house it gradually has struck
me my parents are both dead

as I walk towards my mother she is all the things she
has always been both the anger and the love   the lack
of understanding and the limited understanding
understand her in her life context   what her life was
that I can never know – can we ever know another person's life – my mother her face her familiar feel the
touch of her   the feel of her clothing   the feel of her
hand

   I want life to be familiar I want my mother back I
want her back now and now doesn't respond now will
never respond

   yet she turns to me

what do I do about the yearning
the yearning which aches away up from my belly up
under my
guts up under my ribs the place of it

this is all I will ever have   this dream
ever! can you understand a word like that!

she is present in every older woman that I see
she never seemed old
she has taken off her red coat
she holds out her hands to me
we take hold of each other's hands and I look at her
I look at her for a time in the eyes in a way I never
did when
she was alive
as I hold her
and look at her

Poem for the Dancer

Carol Tilbury

I *found the old photographs*
In the bags and boxes
That I brought back from the house.
They were the ones
I'd half remembered,
Couldn't find after her death,
And suddenly they were there,
Among old school reports, receipts and papers.

'Florrie, aged one year'
My grandmother's writing
Scrawly, on the back.
A little doll-child,
Tiny face surprised at the camera,
Dressed in a bonnet and soft, large coat.

'Florrie, aged two'
Her father proud beside her.
He in his suit and bowler hat,
And she is wearing the same coat,
But now it fits.

School photo.
A shy face, amid forty other girls
Submissively one of many.
Then, two photos of her dancing
In the chorus line.
A row of women
Legs held high,
All trying to look the same.
Long ago I'd marked her with a cross
Needing to know
Which of these glamorous ladies
Was my mother.

Then there's one beautiful picture
When she was twenty-one.
Soft brown hair and eyes
And it is torn
Repaired with lines of sellotape
Making her smile strangely at me.
She'd ripped it all to pieces angrily,
And I, knowing it was too precious to waste,
Had stuck it back together.

My mother and grandmother
Striding along some seaside promenade
And then, a leap of nearly twenty years,
And here am I, a grown daughter,
Sitting on the beach with her at Brighton.
She looks beautiful at sixty
And I look
Exactly like my father,
Who is smiling down at me.

One last picture
Her seventieth birthday.
And in front of her
A table full of food and flowers,
Provided by her children.
But she looks sad here
Out of place
Amid such quantities
And somehow overwhelmed
By all the quiches and the salads.

I stare and stare.
Strange and so familiar face
Of my mother.
I didn't look like you
Or dance like you
Or even
Cook the same food.

Lately we were fighting,
Fighting all the way.
But in the photos you are smiling
And sometimes
You look as though you love me.

Be 'Someone'

Zelda Curtis

Guilt. Overwhelming, painful guilt. It gnawed away at my conscience when my mother died. I tormented myself with unanswerable questions. Could I have helped her more? Perhaps I should have visited her more. Tears flowed, but they couldn't wash away the worry that I had not been able to give her all the love she needed.

I lead such a hectic political life that it was difficult enough to satisfy the demands of my own children let alone those of my mother. Certainly I had limited time to visit her. But how many visits could ever have been enough to counter the loneliness of her last years? Each time a visit ended she would still be left to the mercy of her own thoughts. Apart from my visits to her, every Saturday she spent the whole day in my home. The whole family would have lunch together and then we would go for a walk or a ride to a park. But she needed more than that, she couldn't bear being on her own.

Every morning before I went off to work I would phone her. And however much I would try to cheer her, it was always the same long moan of how empty her life was. That did not start my day off too well. She had the knack of making me feel it was all my fault, though I knew that I could never give her what she wanted.

She made it very difficult for me to know how best to help her, but all too easy to understand how far I fell short of her expectations. She wanted so much love. Only total devotion could suffice, and how many daughters could give that? I think I was as good as most, but I could never have been good enough for her.

No, each day she would remind me of what wonderful daughters her sisters had – they truly loved their mothers. They really cared. They were repaying the debt they owed their mothers for being born into this world. Did I owe a debt? Had she been such a good mother? It's difficult to answer that. Perhaps there were times when I could have answered yes, but so often I would have had to say no.

Perhaps now, sixteen years on, when I am nearly the age she was when she died, and alone and unwell as she was, I can look back on our two lives and their interaction with greater understanding. Perhaps a different perspective will cast a kinder light.

Mum was seventy-two when she died but in her mind her life had been over some years before. It began to ebb with the death of her youngest sister. They had been so very close. I had always felt that her sisters meant more to her than I did. The next blow for her was when Joe died. She and Joe had been living together for ten years or more. My father had died young, many years before, but that had hardly seemed to affect her at all. It had not been a happy marriage. Her years with Joe were stormy too, but she did enjoy his companionship towards the end of his life, and was glad of his caring help.

Then her eldest sister died – and that, as I remember, gave

her some hurtful pangs of guilt. Aunty had become a little confused with age and unable to cope alone in her St John's Wood flat. So Mum had placed her in a Home, but the move only confused her more. She declined fast and her death hit Mum hard. The final blow was her own ill-health. She couldn't come to terms with it, especially as no one seemed able to tell her what was really wrong, despite numerous hospital tests. That's why my very first feeling on her death was of relief that she was spared any further suffering. She had wanted to die, but it had not been an easy death.

When I look back on her life now, I feel great pride in her achievements. She was a strong woman. She had been steeled by the lash of her father's buckled leather belt, burningly felt across her back. She had been hardened by the anti-Semitism she had endured living and working in the East End. Coming to Britain from Russia as a child of eight, speaking only Yiddish, had not been easy. Being a daughter, not a son, made life more difficult. No 'Jewish Princess' was she. My grandfather had been 'blessed' with five daughters, much to his chagrin. But he made them work just as much as any sons he might have had – like workhorses. He was a cabinet-maker and needed the wood brought from the mills. My mother and her sisters had to drag the heavy loads of timber with ropes wrapped around them through the streets of Hackney to his basement workshop. She felt so embarrassed, so ashamed, she told me.

Mum had little formal education and even less encouragement, but she was determined to free herself from poverty and the shame she felt. She wanted wealth. She wanted to be 'someone', and nothing would deter her – not her hasty marriage to my father, an out-of-work furrier, not the too-early birth of her child (me), nor the sudden death of her second child, a son. He had been placed with a wet-nurse so that my mother could go to work, but the milk did not agree with him and he died within a few weeks. After a break of eight years she had two more daughters, one of whom died at the age of eleven.

Night school, studying shorthand and typing, was Mum's route out of the ghetto. She became a secretary. Few Jewish girls in those days made that grade – it was difficult to escape the little backstreet workshops churning out cheap clothing. All her sisters did their stint on the sewing machines, but they too were ambitious. They worked long hours daily and on Sundays they sold broken biscuits on a market stall in Petticoat Lane, until they had saved up enough to start a small millinery business. It wasn't too long before my mother had managed to make enough to open her own shop in Upper Street, Islington.

She had little time for me and yet it didn't seem to worry me – I remember my childhood as happy. The streets were my playground and the little alleys of Upper Street resounded with the tap tap of my ball against their walls. The canal was out of bounds but I still went there, cheekily asking a grown-up to take me across the main road. My favourite was Chapel Street Market, where the coster-women were friendly and generous with their wares. They all bought their funeral hats from my mother's shop.

I saw very little of Mum as the shop opened up at eight in the morning and didn't close until nine in the evening, ten on Saturdays. Even Sunday mornings it opened until two p.m. and then in the afternoon we would go shopping in Whitechapel for the felts and ribbons, the pins and feathers needed for the milliners to work on in the morning.

I loved my mum then. We lived above the shop. After she had closed up at night, she would come up to my room, waken me and feed me with chocolates. But as her fortunes grew and I grew, so did the gulf between us. Her values were not mine. My interests were alien to her. She always used to say she wanted me to be a 'lady barrister' when I grew up. She said it with a laugh, knowing it was really not on for a Jewish girl (Rose Heilbron hadn't made it by then). She hoped I would make a good marriage, meaning that I should marry a man with money. 'A millionaire would be nice,' she'd giggle. Impossible dreams, but how she hoped they could come true! I didn't oblige.

Oh yes, I was a sad disappointment. I didn't fulfil any of her hopes. They were hers, not mine. Her dreams were about what she had wanted for herself. Money and status – to be someone. But to give credit where it's due, she did recognise the value of education and was tremendously proud of me when I passed my matriculation exams. And whilst I may not have ended up as rich as her sisters' daughters – no mink coats or diamond rings for me – she had to admit that I had done better at school. What she couldn't stomach was that my education led me to become a communist. I used my education to work for the Party.

We couldn't talk about it. It hung between us, a huge screen behind which we hid our frustration, anger, disappointment, tears of upset. I tried to love her still, but all our talk was of trivialities, none of our true feelings were ever expressed. She was never directly critical of me, always it was dressed up as commendation of what her sisters' daughters achieved, their wealth, and what they did for their mothers. I could never match up to them.

She could never understand how I could work so hard for so little for the causes I espoused. As an immigrant she had quickly realised that in this country wealth and status were what mattered. Those that had them were the winners and I was one of the losers. What she saw in this country made her decide to be one of the 'haves'. I had aligned myself with the 'have-nots' to fight for a fairer distribution of wealth. She despised me for that.

Her lifestyle was so different from mine. Her values, hopes and goals totally opposed to mine. Yet I still loved her – not the uncritical love of a child for its mother, but a love that accepted her flaws. How I wish she could have accepted mine. Her last few years put greater strains on my love. I found it more and more difficult to accept some of her attitudes. She sapped my confidence, made me feel inadequate. She was always putting me down with her constant comparisons. Nothing I did pleased her. Nothing I said interested her. And the more she accused me of not loving her, the more I felt that I did not.

And as I write this I am aware that you can say she was probably thinking the same – how could she love me when I didn't love her? Why couldn't I see her point of view? I understand that, but we had grown too far apart. After so many years of divergent life-paths, how do you get in step again? Perhaps given time it is possible, but as you get older the years go by all too quickly and somehow there isn't ever the time you need to make good the cracks in your relationships.

I understand how like her I really am, and in a way it has always frightened me. Yet I can think of ways in which I do hope I am like her. After her death I would find myself looking into the mirror to find my mother's face staring back at me. I found myself examining my actions for signs of her in me, and finding them. I found myself checking my relationships with my daughters – and wondering.

Death is real, but I have never believed in it as a parting. My mother is within me and in all my actions. I can see her face in mine and in my mind I can hear her voice and can giggle at some of her funny sayings. 'Aren't you lucky, Zelda' she said when my first daughter was born, 'to have a mother who has had children!' But I also hear some of her less wise sayings coming out of my own mouth sometimes.

It worries me.

My guilt is now assuaged. My anger has gone and time takes away some of the pain. Perhaps I can carry my mother within me more comfortably now, with greater understanding and compassion.

January 20th

Robyn Selman

T he phone rang three thousand miles away.
Marlene said what she said. I said, OK,
softly, as my heart opened wide to try
to hold on to my mother who had died

thirty minutes before. Jan went to work.
I stayed home to pack and choose airline times.
Clouds massed as rain threatened outside.
I made a trip by cab to the doctor's

to pick up a bottle of pills I could
take if things got too much, which they did. I
never did take them three thousand miles
away. The storm came like I said it would.

Jan, not me, was a mess on the plane. We
got to the house thirty minutes before
my brother Michael whose plane came in late
because the storm travelled south and kept

him three thousand miles away. We walked

room to room. *The sun, so beautiful there –*
purple and amber turn the sky pink – set
over the skinny stream three thousand

miles across the street. Nobody else
died that day. Nobody who was famous
who could mark the day. That night in a dream
she asked me for more I couldn't give her.

My mother's sun, her moon, enters and leaves
these rooms. Was Michael a mess? I thought I
wasn't. Did our mother love us? Money
answered what she would not. But thirty minutes

ago we all finally felt close and
I tried to hold on with that long oh... kay
to a love I hadn't let myself lose before
the phone rang three thousand miles away.

YOU were not my Mother

Julie Bellian

I was a 'wanted child'. After two short months – unimportant, lost – you became my mother. And I was very precious to you.

But sometimes you avoided my eyes. Did you keep your secrets there? When I was thirteen I asked you suddenly:

'Mum, have you ever felt like suicide?' (Why did I ask you that?)

'No I've always thought there was a lot to live for,' you said, not looking. But you didn't say what it was that was worth living for. That year you began to conceive your tumour. They aborted it. And you didn't live.

'...Your mother was a saint... you were so precious to her... we never told her she was dying... when you were a baby, they saved you for a good family because you were special... she had no pain... do you have an older woman friend whom you can talk to about boyfriends and things...? Your mother is very sick, you know... cancer can be beaten... if caught in time...'

But you did not want your 'sickness' caught in time. You did not want to fight it, beat it. And anyway, it was doctors and technology that beat cancer. 'Cancer can be beaten,' said the sticker from the Cancer Research Fund on the car window. The affluent suburban wives of successful men gave selflessly their energies, campaigning for good causes such as these. (Tactfully, the sticker was removed on the day of the funeral... my brother crushes it in his fist and tries to smile.)

But it was you who was beaten, though I do not know from what. I read with an irrational fear when I was younger, that 'childless women get it'. Later, I read, this time with recognition, that the risk of cancer developing was greater in people who did not express feelings 'effectively'. Especially anger... I tried to remember you ever being angry.

You were not my mother. Is that why you died? Why you could let yourself die while saying that your 'family' could not go on without you? Knowing that there was no real family of your creation – only a substitute daughter, son... and silent ghosts of desires that had long been stolen from you.

The ghost of the baby you never conceived was displaced in your belly by a tumour – it was so healthy it swelled as you waited for it to go away, keeping yourself from the doctor. You smiled to think you looked six months pregnant. You nurtured it until they cut it out. And then I watched in silence – echoing yours, as you faded away. I watched you vomit from the chemotherapy. Behind hospital doors the invisible heat of radiation painlessly penetrated you. It would cure you, everyone agreed. But at home it turned your urine to fire. In your mild words you described your pain as a red-hot poker. I heard it, forcing itself through you behind another closed door. You quietly let squeeze out a feeble cry behind which lay the scream you never screamed... of pain, of rage, of desire.

What was it that was stolen from you?

I was, I am, so different from you. But I too am a childless woman. I too have stifled my anger to the explosive point of denial. Did I inherit this from you? Learn it? Reproduce it as daughters do? Though it made no sense, at sixteen I feared cancer as the consequence of refusing motherhood; but I knew I could not inherit your cancer, because you were not my mother. But could I engender it through my own lack of feeling? This became my new fear. Swallowed anger, the silent denial that had devoured you. Would this be my fate too? Was I denying something? I searched for anger and seemed to find none.

But it was not anger I could not express. With rage and precision, I slashed myself, but I did not grieve. Silenced at my birth, I did not know how.

Now, I speak of you, and the fact that you are dead leaves me free to open the taboos that held us apart. I do not need to protect you as other daughters must do. Dead, you have nothing now to fear when I speak of sexual abuse, infertility, adoption. When I chase rage and guilt to free them from their hiding places, I open my pain. I look for clues, I fit together possibilities... Sixteen years after not mourning your death, I begin to remember you.

In glimpses of you, I touch a vague and distant grief; and I am close to you within this grief, my mother. I am searching for your story.

Even if I could ask you now – know you, know your past – could this have any relevance to me? Could it help me understand myself, or my life, I who have always felt myself infinitely different from you? In how I look, how I think, how I move... in what destiny I construct, in what wounds, what triumphs I have embraced and consumed and now call MY LIFE.

So different were we that there was no need for me to rebel against you. You were not my mother.

You were not my mother because you did not give birth to me. But you were expected to act as if you had, while explaining to me that you hadn't. But wanting children so badly, you were able to love me just as if I were your REAL child. But I was no one's natural child. As a child I was not even convinced that I had been born 'naturally' at all. I had been chosen, not born. And you had also been chosen – to take on the job of being my mother. Chosen by experts; adoption was organised by rules and by laws. But it was all for love and the good of the child. It was 'scientific' and it was 'moral'; it was even 'natural'. There were no Gods, no accidents, and no mysteries in my adoption story.

You were my mother. I might have been different from other children, yet I was assured I was normal. To me, it was therefore natural that you didn't touch me, that I didn't seek your scent, that I pulled away, that I wanted to sleep alone, that I didn't love you, that I didn't miss you... that I didn't cry when you died...

This was natural.

I knew myself to be a daughter with no real mother. For fifteen years you acted as mothers do and then you died. Without much thought, and even less emotion, I became what I had always been... a girl without a mother. Naturally, because I was born that way. With no mother. Wasn't I?

You had been dead another fifteen years when I began to consider my own female evolution. Feminism, psychology, therapy, even common sense told me I must look to our relationship as mother and daughter to understand my experience and my sense of female self. My conditioning, my behaviour, the construction of my personality, my identity: there were many theories to inform me. I was looking for causes – explanations for the ways I perceived my experience of gender, my sexuality, the contradictions in my values. This was a game with no end, based on questions with no answers. Or too many answers, all possible.

I invested in this, and banished feeling from my world. There was more prestige in 'critical thought', more protection in intellectual distraction. I talked of feelings but did not feel. I perfected the covering of gut rage with angry words. Powerful, rational words. My need to grieve was kept invisible by my denial embodied in these words. My denial was empowered by the lie told in the world about women: YOU HAVE NOTHING TO CRY ABOUT. YOU ARE A LUCKY GIRL, YOU HAVE EVERYTHING. YOU SHOULD BE GRATEFUL. YOU SHOULD BE HAPPY. YOU MUST NOT CRY.

An official letter came: 'I have made contact with your birth mother.'

This lie split me open. My own mind had censored me in insisting truth was unknowable.

But so true was this lie, it hit solidly against my skull. So clear that I laughed an insane laugh at all I had believed in my head in betrayal of my body and I screamed a shaking cry that ejected the lie and shook my body sane.

And people still will say, 'It's because you have found your real mother that you are happy now.'

It is not in finding her, my first mother, alive in the world. But rather in the dissolving of all those myths of mother-love, I am left with my own flesh. In this I found, not a primal truth, but the reality of my pain. Pain denied me to keep me wounded.

To the world my new sanity looks mad as I seem to celebrate my pain by embracing it.

And now I look back on all my theories – my academic interest in Women, in the mother and daughter dynamic. I was trying, through the distancing of intellectual inquiry, to uncover my past, our past. To deconstruct, reconstruct, my personal process.

Whatever this process of becoming a woman is called – by whatever ideology, the assumption is always that girls have mothers. A single, known and tangible mother that functions as a central female figure which the daughter either conforms to or rejects.

(But what about a dead mother? An invisible mother? Two mothers, two dead mothers, a mother back from the dead to rewrite the past by telling a new story?)

Somehow, with and without a mother, I 'became a woman'. Yes, you were my role model because you were the woman I saw when I looked up from the vantage point of your belly as I hung exhausted onto the straps of your shopping bags... Yours were the eyes and the belly I saw before me, solid and real, behind which hovered the abstracted eyes and belly – an elusive memory – of another mother, fifteen years younger than you... Not being imaginatively inclined, preferring the empirical and the rational to fantasy, I pushed that primal mother away with the memory of my birth.

And when I began to grow and menstruate, and as my mind contemplated itself as female, you began to grow your death. Through your death you also became my model for mortality, decay, death... But you were not a gloomy or tragic woman. Neither your life nor your death had even any of that glamour. It was all too clean, too 'painless', to allow me to scream my horror and disgust, to tear YOUR pain out of MY throat. You embodied the lie of the clean and painless death.

You were a mother who never conceived or gave birth. Sterile was a word whispered out of politeness. Your womb was cut from you when you were forty-two. I was a clever little girl who understood that it was the 'part in the stomach where babies are made'. But I knew already that you didn't make babies like other mothers. So you didn't need it, and anyway, it was just one part, like a part in a machine. I understood the logic of machines.

I asked you, home from hospital, 'When they take out an old part, do they put in a new one?' And everyone laughed.

I have never wanted children. You wanted them. The notes in the adoption file – words hidden away for thirty years to keep things 'perfect' – said there was 'no discernible reason for failure to conceive'. But you were lucky, you later got the children you wanted – and not just ordinary children, but 'special' children. As if this were better.

You were my model for the perfection of motherhood.

But you could not model birth... My own birth had become a mythical event. Birth had no reality in flesh and sound and blood and gravity for me or for you. And so it became as light and painless as a metaphor. Even as an idea it was absent in my world. Abstract creativity took its place; it appealed to my imagination which was as clear as thought... not heavy with colours or images. While the birth of my body was mythical and uncertain, my thoughts were real; my consciousness seemed solid to me, seated in my mind where also seemed to sit the power of my will. And both my mind and my will were MY creation. And so from this place, this energy, I believed I could create all I wanted, all I needed.

I had no body.

By twelve, I had turned my inner world outwards and adults looked small; my mind expanded into freedom (and my body fooled the heavy and weak – those men who intruded – who thought that the body they touched was ME.) I felt uncircumscribed by limits: I had not been born like other daughters. I saw your empty belly and knew that you could not prove I had ever been born. You were my mother but you had not made me and therefore had not bound me. You had given me no limits and could give me none because I was not your daughter.

Because you did not give birth, or create anything solely for yourself, I readily embraced the myth that creativity was an intellectual endeavour. It took place in a domain high above the stultifying world of earth and flesh. Identifying with these abstractions, I excited my thoughts and while never calling them 'masculine', I aligned myself, my mind, with the forces that win easily in the world. I believed I could fly from my body, my roots and my beginning, to an imaginary state of disconnectedness.

You did not give me birth. But you gave me the disconnectedness that I turned into freedom. Did you ever believe you had the right to feel I was yours? Did you dare? Suddenly, you had a baby. I was all yours because I had no past. Only a wide open future which you would help to shape.

Yet you were afraid to shape me, to try to form me. Must it be your fear I thank for my freedom?

In the heavy, early morning hush of that sterile house, a man silently pushes my door. He is nice to me. He likes me. He likes all of us, he is 'a friend of the family'. And as he abuses me, I cease to be that child. At some forgotten moment within that vivid yet vague eternity between age nine and thirty, I grow up. As you sleep, there, so far, far away, at the end of the hall.

Can a daughter inherit the pattern of her mother's own childhood abuse? This intrusion would silently steal something from me – my child's desire... my open senses. I closed to pleasure and my body left me. It did not hurt. Was this also you? The deadness underneath the veil of serenity keeps me from knowing the truth of those moments when you DID NOT HEAR YOUR DAUGHTER. My silent 'no', my violated eyes. My evasion of those hands. What kept you away from me all those eternal moments? Were you frozen from fear? Too desperate or too tame a wife? Or, asleep, safely asleep?

...No, like the cancer, I will not inherit this from you – I am not your daughter and I will not die in silent rage.

By not coming to me, down that hall, into those silent mornings, by not knowing, not hearing, not speaking, you prepared me for your death. For the day you would not be there, even in body, for your 'daughter'. You prepared me by being already absent, half-dead in spirit, struggling to animate the burden of a body which had long-ago closed to desire for anything.

And so I ceased to be that child, in order that I would not feel myself die your living death of passive silence, beneath the toxic contempt of that man's force... of any man's force.

Was it in that moment of ceasing that I chose not to take anything from you... anything of yours? I did not have to. I was ADOPTED. I could choose the woman I was becoming.

I can grow taller than you
I will be taller than men
I will grow stronger, wiser, freer
I will out-think them, out-talk them, out-smart them,
out-stare them
I will out-run them
I will face them
My eyes will turn them to stone
My words will wither them
I will do all that you did not do
I will.

Out of your passivity was born my strength. But through the fantasy of perfection that was silently pressed upon us, we were violated. And you disrupted this fantasy yourself so well by dying how and when you did. A lingering death that spanned the crucial years of my adolescence. In this you rebelled and in this I find your strength.

You did not leave me either empty or nostalgic; neither wanting nor fulfilled. You did not leave me the need to create my own daughter 'to recreate the happiness I had' or 'to create the happiness I never had'. Our bond was not one of blood. It was not even the bond of 'family'. It was, and still is, the bond of our shared and separate histories.

As a baby I pulled away from you. As a girl I waved you away, believing you admired my independence. When you died, I walked away, believing myself strong but silently carrying your pain.

And now I carry your desires. You were not my mother, and yet I carry your life in mine. And at last I break the silence – I speak to you.

I believed all you ever told me... I believed that you loved me and in that you gave me the love I had for myself. Your fear became my space for freedom and your distance cemented my fearlessness. Or was it a fearlessness already there; unconscious and unchosen? I have created a mythological story – that I was conceived and born in aweful freedom. But in the history of my body, my beginning, there is only a void. In the void of my past there is no danger. There was a body which could not be sensed; space where no feeling could sound. A hole where your womb once was...

In a void there is no fear. With this fearlessness I pushed against that other womb, and gave birth to myself. A woman with no mother.

Telephone Box in France

Helen Pausacker

Alan stops his bike, and points.
'I can't.'

'You have to,' he says. 'It's a long flight home, and you'll wear yourself out crying for the next three days. You need to find out that everything's all right.'

'No, I need to sit down and have a coffee first. I can't ring without a coffee.' But there are no cafés here. Nothing but a church, a couple of houses and a phone booth. Over the road there's a low wall and behind that the sea stretches out to the horizon. We are in the middle of nowhere, in a town I don't even know the name of. We'll have to go on further to get coffee.

I am procrastinating, but deep down I know he's right. Alan's been a friend of mine for fifteen years. We came out together as teenagers. It was me he first told he was gay, and I've cried on his shoulder when each of my girlfriends has dumped me. And crying is what I've been doing all morning. My eyes are red and puffy, and I can't explain to him what's wrong. I know I'm overreacting.

It started when we went to the post office this morning at Angers to collect our mail from the poste restante, and for the first time I didn't get any letters. Nothing from Sue. I know it's irrational to jump to the conclusion that she's fallen in love with someone else, just from that. And I don't quite believe she has. I didn't get *any* letters, after all...

Obviously there's something wrong with the mail. If Sue hadn't written, then my mother, Sylvia, would have. My mother is very diligent and there's been a chatty postcard from her at each stop, telling me about the weather and bits and pieces of what she's been doing. Girlfriends have dropped me in the past, but mothers never let you down. So intellectually I know there's a mix-up with the mail, but the tears just keep coming. They dripped onto my croissant and into my hot chocolate at breakfast time, and left a little trail for the next ten kilometres.

Alan thinks I'm irrational, I can see that. I'm embarrassed too, but how can I explain to him, that looking at that telephone makes my stomach tie itself in knots? Alan may not understand, but he's kind, and his face is wrinkled with worry.

'Just ring Sue, and say you wanted to check that she's picking you up from the airport. It will calm you down, and stop you worrying.'

I pick up the phone, put my money in and dial. Alan walks tactfully over to the other side of the road and sits on the low wall.

Sue answers, and starts straight away,

'Darling, I've got very bad news for you. I'm sorry to have to tell you like this...'

Doesn't surprise me. I knew something was up. It's all off, that's why she's being nice to me. I'm shaking. I want to tune out for the rest of it. I know how these speeches go. Just get it over.

'Your mother's dead,' Sue continues. 'She's suicided. She went missing for a few days, and they found her on Tuesday.

We've been trying everywhere to contact you...'

It's taking me all my effort to shovel in the five-franc coins. We're going to get cut off. Sue hasn't dropped me after all. Everything's all right. I was just imagining things... No, it's not all right. She said my mother was dead. But my mother can't be dead. I'm imagining things. I'm going mad. I'm sobbing. What can I say? And I'm running out of five-franc pieces. I can't stand up much longer in this phone booth. It has spider webs with dead insects stuck on it. My legs are shaking. And my mother's killed herself?

'I'll ring back in five minutes or so. I need to stop now. Alan is with me.'

When I hang up, my legs give way, and I collapse. I can't work out how to stand up. Alan runs over to see what's going on. There's a man waiting to use the phone, and he looks shocked. I can't think of any French words to apologise and tell him what's happening. It's confusing enough trying to tell Alan.

It's not that Sylvia had always been happy, but she was always interested in people, doing things, trying hard to work life out. She'd seemed happier in the last six months, calmer, as if she'd found something. I'd stopped worrying about her.

'I saw her just before we left,' Alan confirms. 'She seemed younger. I can't believe it.'

Neither can I. I'm sitting here with my trousers rolled up, and the sun beating down on me. We're on holiday. Australia is on the other side of the world. Perhaps I misheard. But gradually it sinks in, and I know that was what I was crying about before. I just couldn't work it out.

Practicalities are difficult in a strange country. We don't have many coins left, and can't work out how to ring reverse charges. But there's a phone number in the booth, which we give to Sue when I ring her back.

I am standing in the middle of nowhere and a phone box is ringing, with a call from Australia. Everything is surreal. Nothing is how it should be.

My family is at Sue's, and they fill me in with the details. How no one had seen my mother since Friday, and my sister Fran had got a letter from Sylvia, saying she couldn't go on any longer, and that she was going walking and where she was. And how they'd contacted the police, who'd sent a search party and found her sitting under a tree, having taken an overdose. Fran reads me the letter Sylvia wrote, but the sounds of the cars and trucks make it difficult to hear it properly, and my brain is suffering from overload. Fran says she wishes I was there.

Couldn't Sylvia have waited till I was home, so I could have been there with Fran? I am useless here, but I can't get home earlier. Almost a week has gone by now, anyway, with my mother lying in a fridge, waiting till I get back as planned on Tuesday. But now it'll be for the funeral.

There's a woman outside. She's been hanging round for a while now. I make faces at Alan so he'll explain the situation to her, but he's done nothing. Maybe his French isn't good enough.

'I have to go now,' I say. 'Someone's waiting to use the phone.'

There are little children riding round on bikes.

'Speak English?' they say and giggle.

I want to scream, but here is not the place. My mother might be dead, but I can't go to pieces yet. I have to get my wobbly legs to cycle at least twenty kilometres for somewhere to stay. There are things to organise. Half the world to travel across. I have to hold together. For the time being. For the rest of my life.

Now, I'm back in Australia. Sylvia's postcard has been returned with all the rest of the mail that got lost in the French mail system. It's sitting on my mantelpiece and has a picture of an Indian rajah on a horse and someone walking behind him with a fan. Sylvia writes, '...I'm sending you a horse and someone to fan you whenever you get tired and hot.'

The others have told me all about the place that Sylvia died in. They say it's calm and peaceful, and it made them feel a lot better to see it.

I don't want to go. I have a vivid memory of where Sylvia died, and it wasn't under a tree, in a beautiful green rainforest. It was in a telephone booth in France.

John Lennon is dead:
In Memoriam

Norma Cohen

John Lennon is dead. Ten years later, I'm listening to him on the radio: *Lennon, The Remembered Years*, a ten-part serial. I'm lying down on the carpet, knees hunched up, smoking a cigarette. The tears slide down my face. I'm remembering my childhood, the dark days. The bus swinging round the corner at Penny Lane, the ding ding of the conductor, the bright lights, the Cavern, the Mersey Tunnel. Us kids flinging ourselves down the gangway, screaming along with the seagulls, racing on to the ferry boat, the *Royal Iris*, 'Waiting to take you away...der der der dum... Waiting to take you away'... across the seas to New Brighton, home of the jellyfish and the candyfloss stalls, even in winter. Llandudno, Costa Brava of the chilly north, us kids buttoned up against the cold, me hips a-sway in my school blazer, the boys in crested caps: Crinny Addy Primary School, Old Swan, posing, football-swollen under their jackets, for Dad's photo, the rain pouring down, the wind howling, me mother headscarved and freezing, pretending to smile...

That frown riddles its way down the years and thirty years later is all I have left of her. Me, looking up into the camera with a sulky face, huddled into a river bank at Ravenglass, Cumberland, the vanished county. The boys dancing strange, war-like poses and screeching smiles, my mother standing behind me, mirroring my stare. *Woman Frowning*, it could have been, or rather, *Mother and Daughter Frowning* after Rubens' *Girl Playing* or *Nymph Singing With Joy*. Her in a stripy dress at Southport on the slatted pier, me with my dad and a brace on my teeth, eyes down, grinning, she sipping lemonade through a straw, face darkened, far away.

'How can I give love when love is something I ain't never had?'

My mother never sang and when she did, it made your heart cry: 'Oh, Pretty Polly Oliver went walking one day...' the sound would waver from her throat, tumbling back through the years, as though she too was crying with the pain of it all. When she got to the bit where the young woman dropped her basket of apples and the man left her singing, I'd bite my lip and pretend not to listen till my ears sung their own dull cry, so angry was I that she'd got me, tickled my sadness, hooked into my heart and dribbled it with pity for her and knowing she wanted me to make it all right, to comfort her, to take charge, to be her mother and her father who'd walked out when she was eleven, never to return.

And – as if that wasn't enough – wanting me to be her husband as well, who in today's psycho-jargon would be called The Absent Father, selling his quire of *Daily Workers* nights, for he was a communist. Absent at union meetings, AWOL from 1945 onwards, bemoaning the camaraderie and freedom of air-force days he'd never smelt since. You could say it was gross irresponsibility, him with three kids to support and slipping out quietly to spend it on the slot machines and later, in his seventies, at the casino. My mother, meantime, holding the purse strings tight, cutting up the orange into three portions that made us squabble. We all wanted the roundie and shied away from the middle bit, the fleshy circle thrown round like a marble till it was too dirty and mangled to hold. Then we'd wait for her wrath and the wet teacloth and swallow it silently, retching on the sticky peel.

John Lennon is dead, like our childhood, rolling down the hill to Princes Park at Eastertime, mangled in laughter. Perhaps it had never ever come alive in the first place. We were born fully grown, well versed in the arts of conversation and political agitation, booklearning and essay writing, passing exams and winning prizes, organising meetings and being The Chair. Our house was organised, in fact, like a Party meeting, me the Chairman (this was before the days of Chairpeople), Dad the Secretary, little Philip in the far corner taking minutes, my elder brother opting out disgusted and quiet before we'd even started, My Mother, as ever, silently pursing her lips, sighing and huffing, resolutely not speaking...

'So I never said a word, I just kept my mouth tight *shut*...' as though this was due some kind of credit.

'Point of order, Mr Chairman,' I'd say, talking to myself, raising my hand and looking straight at my father, 'but don't you think it's about time you and Mum got a divorce, what with all that shouting and us kids hanging around half the night at the top of the stairs?'

'I don't think that's an appropriate item on the agenda for this meeting, thank you,' said Dad, stiffening and shaking out his initialled handkerchief, perfectly and uselessly creased down the centre with a firm iron by his wife, sneezing theatrically five times and then blowing his lungs out to change the subject. The school whistle at half-time. We'd sit there like Mum, swallowing down the bitterness, the unresolved personal question, the Big Issue: Why weren't we ordinary like everyone else? Perhaps that's why I married someone ordinary – at first glance at least – to escape the strain of being intellectual and morally pure and sexless (sex, a word never mentioned in our house, except for *Married Love* by Herbert Read, hidden under the bookshelves and only lent out to married comrades in some unmentionable difficulty). Letting myself off the hook...

John Lennon is dead. I know that for a fact, because the day I went round to see my friend John Burrows he had a ten-foot blow-up photo of him on his kitchen wall. And now I know he's dead, and it still seems to matter in my heart of hearts. Because then we were all children of the sixties, that ten-year lost weekend, we could do what we liked, the world was our oyster, we would live forever on the welfare state and the dream that the future was ours and all we had to do was to use our imagination and all our longings of hope and love and freedom would come true.

I know that's not true now, because our world has become a big market place and we got off the boat too quickly and now we don't have the money or the power to buy anything in the market any more. Ten years ago, we'd wander round the markets of Islington and the East End, eagle-eyed, sneaking out bright bits of old junk and musty clothes and eat Sundays at Blooms down Whitechapel, the hot beigels and cream cheese rolling in our bellies and reflected in our clear eyes. We're still children of the sixties, living in the nineties where the Dream is Over and the world seems a chilly place.

And now I can't cry for my mummy any more because my mummy's dead and I have become a mummy, pointing out the bright future to my daughter, in the same secret breath acknowledging that I also can't live forever. I'm standing on the bridge. All things must pass. I too will die and someone else with the same laughing eyes and determined step will have to take the bright torch on for me.

I know John Lennon is dead because I saw his death replayed over and over on the television screen ten years later, the newscaster hanging in to capture the very moment, the shot, the hushed faces crowding into the New York block, the reported whisper... 'Please help me.' I know he's gone because Yoko said so, lounging quietly with Sean in the white flat near the white piano and the white cushions looking at the movie some sharp mogul had made to commemorate his death, the pundits wrestling with the new, fashionable theme: Was he, in fact, so important after all, and if not, why not?

I know he's dead because nobody gets dressed up in paper bags any more – at least not in public, waving a flag and two fingers at the Vietnam war and saying, 'This is peace, man,' the exiled Liverpudlian coming home to New York to spill out his dark dreams.

I know he's dead because when the papers scream out eagerly 'Top War Ministers Have Urgent Meeting on the Gulf', there's no one to sing a different tune.

'What's the Gulf, Mummy?' asks my daughter, swooping her head round the living room door.

'It's... it's...', I reply.

How can I offer junior politics when I'm thinking, 'Yes I'm scared too but there's no time for fears here.' I've got to pretend the world will last for ever as I did when I was young, even through Aldermaston and the Cuban missile crisis and sitting in a newsreel cinema that felt like a bunker and everyone saying, 'We're on the Brink.' No matter that with a heightened thrill of reality I marched along with the best of them, rainy and cold to Aldermaston, to the church where Macmillan drove up in a Rolls with Kennedy and we saw his sun-tanned, smiling face. Then we were fourteen or fifteen, and it was only another five years later when we were standing on the gravel at a remote college hostel in outer Surrey that Pat Gibbins was saying proudly, 'I'm a Catholic like he was.' We'd just been stunned by the news of Kennedy's death over the radio and thirty years later I recall in slow motion the drugged paralysis that gripped us all, the frame that stopped our lives: where I stood, where he stood, where she stood as we swallowed the first big shock of our lives.

My grandmother dying seemed kids' stuff after that as we all laughed hysterically through the four-hour train ride to Liverpool, to the funeral, the covered mirrors, the prayers, the ten-bob note slipped silently into my hand by a gentle uncle. The lines on my dad's face – no tears, no sentiment when his father had died, terrified to meet his Maker, a few years before.

And then... sliding back even further to that terrible moment when I was five. We were walking gaily along the street with my friend Miriam, who lived in our house, when out she ran, urgently and suddenly from my grasp, without warning, in front of a bus, a red double-decker, and was killed. The body all bloody, seeping into the tarmac, the old man shouting angrily at the crowd pressing forward, the gasps, he running now, covering her body with his overcoat, laying her out hurriedly along the counter at the dry-cleaners' next to Wallers, the cream cake shop. The cake shop lady walking us home round the corner to Bentley Road and asking us what we were going to have for dinner.

'Hot pot,' I'd said under my breath, as we climbed the stairs to our top-floor flat, the smell of cooked meat turning my stomach without knowing why. Thirtysomething years later, I wanted to call my own daughter Miriam, but didn't dare in case it revoked the curse. Breathing in hard when she was five years old, never letting go of her hand, squeezing it tight until she was six.

'What are you thinking, Mummy?' she'd say, as the squeeze involuntarily got tighter.

'Nothing, darling,' I'd laugh. 'Just... things...'

She'd not been convinced. And then, finally, five years later...

'Is Grandma really going to die?' she'd asked, looking up at me directly as we walked to the sweet shop.

'Yes, darling, I think she might,' I'd replied, lying hard about the might but proud of my half-honesty, found only recently with the aid of New Age therapy books.

And then the bright, night-time lights at Victoria Station, making those fateful journeys to Hove, to the hospice where my mother lay dying, paralysed, staring at the ceiling.

'Now let's get down to brass tacks. Am I going to die?' she'd asked, my brothers and I gathered round her bedside on her sixty-ninth birthday, the birthday cake in crumbs on the sheet. The side table stacked with cards and flower jugs, the revolving whirr of *The Fiddler on the Roof* providing the awkward link between them, him clutching the bottle of champagne, the clasped hands, the 'I love you, my darling,' the words of endearment they'd never exchanged in a lifetime.

'It's worth it,' she'd said, beaming bravely up at us all as Dad sat there stiff and gaunt and speechless, the tears welling up somewhere down his jacket, the rigidity of a man who'd never given way to his feelings in a lifetime except for the sob, the stifled cough in the kitchen as he'd stumbled for a moment before buttoning up again and standing up straight, his back cricking as he leant against the kitchen roll nailed to the wall.

And then the slow walk through the green lawns, the flowers arranged in neat rows... Beloved daughter of Augustus Edward Jones and Bessie Bernstein, all our fondest memories, your loving grandchildren, and our measured paces through the snapping twigs, the cold winter air on our cheeks, us linking arms with my father in the way you saw other people's families do. We'd never been so close as now as we all moved silently to the spot: Bed number six, row f. We searched for our mother's empty plot with its brown, plastic headstone: Eve Cohen, teacher, communist and friend to all who knew her, beloved wife of... The undertaker with his ridiculous hat and shiny suit, the gravedigger from a bad production of *Twelfth Night*, he'd even got the funeral march wrong, coming in five beats too late after the Schubert and the live flute... bent frame sticking out from behind the black curtain as he ticked out the minutes on his stopwatch and clicked on the tape recorder in full view of the congregation. Respectfully waiting a moment before he upturned the urn, Aladdin's lamp with a silly spout, and we watched the burnt grey ash pour out silent and airborne before floating down to the damp earth, the last few drops making us cough as he dutifully shook out the remaining specks as if he were knocking out a teapot. My dad finally cracked, for a moment faltering, and we adult children caught him on our shoulders, tightening round him, protecting his seventy years, supporting him in our quiet ring, looking ahead at the skyline with the sound of lorries roaring dimly away.

And then the mood breaking, him stooping to plant the rosebush: Fison's Eveline, funnily enough. Sheer coincidence, I suppose, that her name was Evelyn too – though she'd never have it and we'd always called her Eve. She'd refused the rabbi and the prayers, dying angrily, staring straight ahead, bloated by the steroids and ageing rapidly over six weeks into an ancient grandmother before our eyes.

And now John Lennon is truly dead, because he'll never come back and neither will my mother whom I silently

wrestled with and shied away from for all her worries and
her fears and her longing for warmth and to be looked after
and to go ballroom dancing and excavating on a dig.

'I'll write it all down, Mum,' I'd said, hunching over the
tape recorder week after week, trying to catch her every
breath, the shakily framed words, her suspicions of the
hospital staff, her acute and upsetting fears about her own
children.

'We're fine, Mum,' we'd said. 'We can cope. You'll always
be with us.' 'I love you more than anything in the world,' I'd
said, believing it then, and she'd carried on the half-untruth,
repeating the words like a litany.

'Look after her, won't you, Mark?' she'd said. 'She's had
such a hard time of it,' as I stood there groaning and laughing for the irony of it all in her throwaway truth.

If only you'd had a Good Death, I murmur two years later
(it's November 17th, her birthday), drinking in Simone de
Beauvoir's memoir to her own mother's passing, *A Gentle
Way of Dying* for a crumb of unravelling.

'C'mon baby, now work it all out...,' John Lennon shouts
from the new red ghetto-blaster. The sounds swing through
the bathroom and my daughter takes up the refrain, rockin'
and rollin' in her own way, tolerating the shift from
Madonna and Phil Collins to give her old fogey mum her
moment of nostalgia. She, careless with the toss of youth in
her lap, her pony-tail madly swinging in the mirror, slicking
back her eleven-year-old 'Hint of a Tint Chestnut' rinse
with the He Man gel.

'Twist little girl... You know, you twist so fine...'

So maybe John Lennon isn't so dead after all. Shake it out
baby. Ah ah ah.

Where's Ma?

Gail Chester

As my mother's disease has progressed, she has taken to asking after her parents.

'Where's Ma? Is she upstairs?'

'Where's Da? Will he be back soon?'

What do you say? How do you answer such questions in a culture which teaches you to ignore death, to pretend it isn't happening, or where the reality can't be avoided, that it was an embarrassing mistake?

Without discussion, my father and sister and I have come to the same conclusion – lying to my mother is not appropriate. So we tell her the truth, each in our own style – my sister haltingly and apologetically, my father kindly and circuitously.

'Where's Ma?' she asks me.

I take a deep breath. 'She's dead.'

'Really,' says Mum, with a startled expression in her eyes, 'when did that happen?'

'A long time ago. Over thirty-five years ago, when I was a little baby.'

'Thirty-five years ago? That's terrible. Why didn't anyone tell me? I never knew. So where is she now?'

'In Bournemouth. She's buried in the cemetery there. You know, you used to go and visit her grave.'

'Isn't that terrible? So she's dead, you say. Why didn't I know?'

In the early days of this conversation, Mum often got angry in the middle of it, as if I were accusing her of unforgivable stupidity.

'It's not Ma I'm asking you about, it's someone else,' she would say pointedly. Maybe this was sometimes true.

'Who then? Who are you asking me about? Moll? She's in America. Meelia? She's at home.'

Mum watched with aggravation as I poked through the list of likely relatives. 'I forget,' she would say.

Often, her anger would focus on the cruelty of her condition. 'How can you tell me she's dead, when I think she's upstairs?'

'Because, I'm afraid, she is dead.'

'How long has she been dead?'

'More than thirty-five years. Since I was a little baby.'

'That's a very long time ago. So why do I think she's upstairs?'

'Because your memory has got bad, Mum. You can't remember things that have happened to you recently. That makes your brain fill up with memories from long ago.'

'So, Ma's dead. That's terrible, I wish I'd known.' A moment's silence. 'And where's Da? Is he outside?' Another pause, a resigned, rebellious look. 'I suppose he's dead, too.'

On Yom Kippur, the Day of Atonement, we were sitting in the kitchen, Mum and I. I couldn't get her to go to shul, but she knew it was a significant day – a day for reflection.

'I don't feel so good,' she said, 'and the world's in a terrible state.' Pause. 'Where's Ma?'

'She's dead.'

'But where is she?'

'She's in Bournemouth, in the cemetery.'

A very, very, long silence, my mother meditating on the tablecloth pattern. Suddenly, she looked up at me across the table, 'Where do people go when they die?' she asked.

I almost laughed. Small children ask such questions, not elderly parents. But clearly, she was concerned not only for her mother.

'Well,' I said, 'there are two main schools of thought on this subject. The first is that when you die, you get buried in the ground and that's the end of it. The second is that when you die, your body gets buried, but your soul leaves your body and goes to heaven, to join the others that have gone before. You can choose whichever theory you prefer.' I decided not to complicate matters at this point by references to cremation, hell or atheism. I think I made the right decision, as Mum looked thoughtful and said, 'I see. Thank you.'

It is very upsetting.

To tell someone four or five times in an afternoon, maybe more, that their parents are dead, have been dead for many years, when each time it comes to them as a distressing new discovery – more than once I have wanted to cry for the sheer misery of the repetition. But what is the alternative? To further confuse a mind struggling to hang on to reality? To let my mother believe her parents are alive, and then what? She will only want to know why they don't come and see her, while occasionally she grasps perfectly well that they are dead. No, in her case, lying is not appropriate.

The other week, Dad was talking to Mr Rosenthal. The Rosenthals belong to the same shul as my parents, they are about the same age. Mr Rosenthal grew up in the East End and was in the army during the Second World War. Mrs

Rosenthal grew up in Poland and survived the Lodz ghetto. Most of her relatives died in the Holocaust. And now Mrs Rosenthal has Alzheimer's Disease.

'What do I tell her when she asks for her parents?' Mr Rosenthal says to my father. 'I can't bring myself to tell her the truth, so I lie.'

Mr Rosenthal has another problem – he doesn't speak a word of Polish. When Mrs Rosenthal was well, her hatred of the Poles was such that she would refuse to acknowledge that she knew a word of their language. But now, in her illness, she frequently reverts to the tongue of happy childhood memories. And she is furious with her husband's stupidity when he does not reply. She thinks he is doing it deliberately, to punish her. Somebody, after all, must be responsible for all this suffering.

My mother died three years ago, three days before my fortieth birthday, after being diagnosed as having stomach cancer a few months before. She'd already been suffering from Alzheimer's Disease for six years. I was not sorry that she got cancer, as it meant that she died without completely losing control of her mental and bodily functions, and while she still recognised my father and sister and me. I am very grateful for that. I am also glad that my mother and I loved and respected each other, both before and during her illness. We had our disagreements – mostly about marriage and Zionism – but when she died there was no unfinished business between us. I haven't been obliged to heap guilt and anger on top of grief and loss.

I admired my mother tremendously for her wonderful perseverance during all the long years of her illness, though sometimes it might have been less painful for us if she had been prepared to let go sooner. In the last year of her life, my mother got stomach cancer. I felt she was suffering from something more than just Alzheimer's Disease, before the cancer was discovered. She had already had Alzheimer's Disease for so many years that it was a source of constant amazement to me that she communicated as well as she did, even while dying of cancer.

She encouraged me to communicate, too. Her one regret about my education was that I refused to take English 'A' level. But I have taken up writing, anyway. And now I find myself writing about my mother, about continuity, about the respect and love she felt for her mother, who also died of Alzheimer's Disease. Throughout her life, and by her example, my mother taught me vital lessons about how to be a strong, proud Jewish woman, never giving in, never turning back. I miss her.

Three-dimensional pictures

Lynden Easterbrook

My father brought me and my brother up on his own, and took a positive attitude towards the future, rather than crying about the past. This was in some ways difficult for me because it meant I never really cried about my mother's death, and therefore never accepted it fully. It is only now that some of the feelings are beginning to emerge.

My mother died in 1959 when I was five, so I only have disjointed snatches of memory about her. Since then different incidents suddenly bring it back to me.

1990

In the yoga class I'm sitting opposite a young woman, staring into her eyes, finding everything else growing more and more blurred, till all I can see is those strong clear eyes. Then suddenly from deep inside comes a great yearning, and tears start pouring out of my eyes. It's Alice's funeral tomorrow. One of my mother's closest friends.

1955

Mummy's on the phone from the hospital, asking me what colour jelly sweets I would like. I start dribbling.

'Some green ones, some orange ones, some yellow ones, some red ones... oh, and some white ones.'

Next time Daddy visits her he brings back a little bag with them in. It's nearly the whole packet. She can't have eaten many.

Sitting in the car outside the hospital with my brother. He's meant to be doing his homework, and I'm meant to be looking at a book. We're not; we're giggling. Two women walk past, and one of them says, 'Look at those two dear little boys.' We giggle helplessly. Don't they know I'm a girl?

Mummy's in bed when I get back from my first visit to the dentist. I go running up to her bedroom and wake her up to show her my first filling. She can't see it, even though I open my mouth wide and put it right in her face. She gets a bit cross. I feel terribly sad and hurt, but I try not to show it.

Christmas Day. Daddy has wound strings all over the house and we have to follow them to find our presents. My strings end up under Mummy's bed. She lies there and watches me opening my presents. I'm excited and happy.

It's not Christmas and it's not my birthday, but Mummy calls me and my brother into the sitting room and gives us a present each. Strange-looking wooden things. 'They're not aeroplanes,' she says. 'They're called stereoscopes. You put double pictures in them and you can see things in 3-D. As though you're really in the picture. My great grandfather made them, and took some of the photographs.' She's gone through the pictures writing our names on each one so that we've both got the same, and don't argue. They're lovely. I like the snow scenes best. I don't understand why she's given them to us now, though.

I'm sitting in front of the gas fire in Mummy's bedroom, talking to her. She's in bed. It's winter, and it's dark outside. It feels so cosy and safe and warm in here.

I'm jumping up and down on my bed, trying to do somersaults. I'm pretending I'm in a circus, and I'm really excited. Daddy comes in. He's very cross.

'Why aren't you asleep? You've woken Mummy up. Don't you realise she's very ill?'

No, I didn't know she was ill. I wonder what's wrong with her.

Daddy, my brother and I are wrapping up a present for Mummy for Mother's Day. It's two bars of Lily of the Valley soap in a lovely box. We don't usually give her a present for Mother's Day, but Daddy says it's nice to because she's in hospital. I write my name on the card.

Sitting in the bath, I'm staring at the wall, and at the flannels hanging on the rail. I should be facing the taps. Daddy doesn't know which way round to put me. How can you lean back against the taps? He's gone down to answer the phone. He's back, rushing me out of the bath.

'Mummy's very ill,' he says. 'The hospital says she may even die.'

'Don't be silly.' Why can't I play in the bath? And why won't he sing to me like Mummy does?

My brother and I have breakfast on our own that morning. Squabbling and kicking each other a bit. Then he's back again. Walking into the room, saying, 'Mummy's dead.' I laugh. 'You're joking.' I can't believe him at all. The laugh on my face starts to freeze.

Then we're rushing not to be late for school.

A few days later Daddy comes in with some things the hospital have given him. There's the lovely box with one bar of Lily of the Valley soap and the crumpled wrapper from the other one. I feel as though my insides are falling apart.

Dim, dim memory of crying and shouting at Daddy, 'You can't throw away her stockings. You can't throw away her nightie and dressing-gown. Please, not her dressing-gown.'

A girl at school asks me what it's like at home now that my mum's dead. Absolute terror. What on earth can I say? How does she know? I grin a frozen grin and say, 'All right.' I mustn't cry. I walk away quickly.

I'm ten, and I dream that Daddy's opening a wardrobe. He says he hid Mummy in it for a surprise, and she's not really dead at all. I jerk awake, and burst into tears. I think it's the first time I really understand that she's not going to come back.

I'm eleven, and at a new school. Nobody knows my mother's dead. The others are all talking about home, their parents. I keep avoiding the subject. I'm getting friendly with a girl called Rachel.

We're late leaving school one day, and she's gone upstairs to get a book. I stand at the bottom of the stairs, trying to work out how to tell her about my mother. Somehow, I'll have to sound casual.

I mustn't cry. I start to practise.

'Oh, by the way, my mother's dead.'

'Oh, didn't I say? My mother died when I was five.'

I suddenly realise she's walked down the stairs and she's standing behind me, listening. I feel so embarrassed at being caught talking to myself, so upset at what I was saying, that I just grin at her. Neither of us ever mentions it again.

I'm fourteen, and I've come home from school alone, feeling terrible. I don't seem to fit in with anyone at school. It's hot and sunny outside, and children go laughing past the house on their way home. Why don't I feel like them? I go up to my room and sit on the bed. Then I get the stereoscope and pictures from the back of my wardrobe, and take them out of the old discoloured plastic bags. I sit going through the pictures one by one. I'm not consciously thinking anything, but gradually I feel my mood change, and tension and sadness drop from my body. A light, happy feeling grows inside.

And over the years, sometimes looking through the drawer

of her things in my father's room. A few letters, her lipstick, her powder compact, a red filmy scarf that still smells of her perfume. The box with the Lily of the Valley soap in.

When I'm thirty-six, my father gives me a file of her letters to sort out. I find a letter written to me when she was in hospital. The page is divided into four squares, and each contains a picture with a word written underneath.

It was written in 1955 when I was two. The pictures are carefully drawn. There are two kisses in pencil after her name.

1990

There are so many people at Alice's funeral that we have to stand at the side, pressed back against the wall, with about

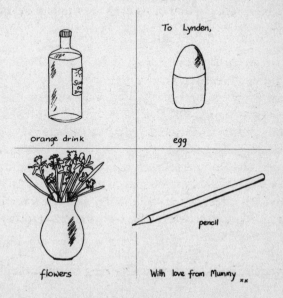

orange drink

To Lynden,

egg

flowers

pencil

With love from Mummy xx

twenty people standing in front of us. We haven't got any hymn books. I'm all right until the second verse of the first hymn. I knew the words of the first verse. Then I stop singing and start looking around.

I suddenly see her husband and daughters. Paula's singing away with all her heart, and she's crying. Tears start streaming down my face. My father's standing next to me. I turn my head away slightly, hoping he won't see. Why do I still feel ashamed of crying in front of him?

The next day I go to see Ruth, and she puts her arms round me. 'You can be yourself here,' she says. 'It's all right to cry.' I feel a wonderful sense of relief, and just sob and sob. Will I ever stop?

Singleton Park

Jo Hughes

Years ago I knew a woman who introduced herself as an orphan. She was in her middle forties and wore a dazzling streak of white hair at her temple. She told me that her hair had turned to white the morning her mother died; she was thirteen at the time. I thought it strange that she should still call herself an orphan at an age when so many of her contemporaries also had dead parents. I thought it wrong somehow, like a deliberate and misguided attempt to draw sympathy. In other words, I thought that because it had now become a common experience for her generation it was somehow extinct.

Three years later my mother died suddenly and I felt the pain as keenly as if I had been ten or fifteen years younger. The sense of loss has not grown any weaker with time; the progression of my life has in some ways been a series of regrets for everything I've done that she has never seen or known about.

Everything I did was for her. I was the spit of her and I worshipped her. I was hers while my sister was my father's, in my eyes. All my drawings were received with unadulterated wonder and praise, nothing was done and finished until her scrutiny made it perfect. In honesty she was without discrimination.

When my mother died I knew that I could never return to the past of her comforting arms, her enveloping softness. The door to her love was shut forever, I could never step back in time and become a child again. When her heart stopped beating, two lives were lost: mother and daughter died, for without a mother can there be a daughter?

There is a large park in the town that I come from, bounded at one end by the hospital and on the other by a church. There are several entrances and therefore different routes that may be followed through it. As a child my father would take me for walks that sometimes led down by the side of the vicarage and passed through the botanical gardens. From there we'd walk past the pond, to the boating lake that lay at the furthest end, dwarfed by the modern complexes of both university and hospital as we went. As a child the imposing and scattered tower blocks and outbuildings of those seats of learning and medicine held mystery for me. I would look upon their myriad windows hoping for a glimpse of a patient or a student performing whatever ritual their respective states of being required. I never thought of the hospital as a place of unhappiness, rather it was to me a place of healing and renewal, of doctors with twinkling eyes and softly spoken nurses, and tasteless, painless medicines.

For eighteen years the park and its environs figured largely in my life; it was the short cut to the sea and the fair. A place of huddled desires and fumbling fingers, a place for hiding in. Solitary walks and rain, ice-cream and boredom, a place marked with the paths of many memories as though my feet have trodden the tale of my growing in the very tarmac and gravel I walked over time and time again.

Our house was not very far from the park's uppermost

entrance. I would walk up a hill and down a hill and down further still to reach its main gates. I used to dream of it as one would dream of a house with many rooms, there was path upon path and places of both danger and safety. I do not dream of it any more; it has passed from centrality in my life to become a seldom remembered haven. Yet if it no longer existed I should feel its loss, I should hunger for it as I hunger for that lost self who played good and bad games there, the root of me that became a stem, grew wild, grew old and left town.

If I return and walk through the park again I will, with my footsteps, mark out the stages of her life. Here, the hospital where she died, where I last saw her. Here, the graveyard where she's buried that I have never since visited. Here, the dark paths and secluded places she warned me of. And here an orphan walking with her daughter, wishing impossible wishes and lamenting the lost one still.

Learning to Scream

Suzanne Bosworth

Her death has been the most liberating experience that I have ever known, although not without its pathos and irony. It was almost Christmas, but she had not been seen for about three weeks. She was found dead on the floor in the bedroom, from a heart attack, lying next to an overturned chair with its stuffing scattered all over the carpet. Piecing the clues together, it was evident that she had intended going away somewhere. She needed the chair to reach the top of the wardrobe. Because on top of the wardrobe was an empty suitcase.

The suitcase that had once imprisoned her daughter.

If you are
    frequently shut up in a suitcase when you are a baby, because you are hungry and screaming for food, you quickly develop a deep-seated fear of the dark and a terror of suffocation. In effect you are stifled because you also learn not to scream.

If you continue

to be physically and emotionally abused and deprived throughout your childhood and beyond, the pain of realising that the people who are supposed to be your carers do not in fact care, is too acute to bear. So you take the guilt upon yourself; you assume that you are being treated in this way because you deserve their anger, and your sense of worth diminishes to nothing.

It is the only way that you can possibly survive.

The realisation that my mother abused me as a baby came to light in therapy only recently; a revelation which marks the beginning of the end of a long cycle of deep unhappiness. I feel that my life is only now beginning at the age of thirty-eight, and although there are still times when hope and courage fail me, equally there are times when I know with an absolute certainty that the rest of my life will be rich and full and worth the living.

I don't remember much of my first few years. The first clear memory is on my sixth birthday. I was playing a game under the table, and stood up suddenly, banging my head hard. I began to cry; my mother hit me and I cried even more, so she hit me again, harder, telling me not to be so stupid.

I was always afraid of her. It was like living with a time-bomb – never knowing when she would lash out for misde-meanours both real and imagined. She knew that I could never retaliate, so she took out all her frustrations and anger on me. My father was still out in Malaya with the Territorial Army – my mother and I had come back early for some reason that I believed to be my fault. How else could I account for the beatings and the bashings and the absence of any love or affection towards me?

And then there he was in his uniform, home. I clung to his neck, sobbing, until I was forcibly taken away from him and put to bed. I was in the way. Bad girls don't deserve any love.

I don't remember him ever hugging me again.

Certainly my mother never hugged me. When I was ill, or when I hurt myself, I expected and got more pain from being hit. My first memory of someone being gentle and kind was at junior school, when a woman bathed my grazed knee and had me laughing nervously through my tears as she dabbed the purple antiseptic on in the shape of a little violet.

I never felt that I belonged at home. I was an intruder, a nuisance, messing up her life and getting in the way. Even my bedroom gave me no sanctuary. Not being allowed to have a bath more often than once a week, I would wash in the handbasin in my room. At ten I was becoming embarrassed by my pubic hair and my breasts growing. I can still remember the humiliation of her leaning against the door, laughing and making fun of my body as I stood naked and shivering by the sink.

Shortly after this, while we were on holiday, I started menstruating. I was terrified. I thought I was dying. But death seemed even more terrifying than the certainty of my mother's anger and I braved my parents' room across the hall. She didn't dare hit me in front of my father, so she dragged me back into my room where she left me in no doubt that I was disgusting and dirty. I had proved myself to be an inconsiderate little nuisance once more – now she had to go and buy sanitary towels for me. So bulky for my small frame that they showed prominently through my swimsuit. Tortured with shame and embarrassment, I begged to wear a skirt to hide everything but she wouldn't let me. Instead I displayed to the world the fact that I was disgusting and dirty.

It was impossible to tell my father that she abused me – she told me often enough that if I did I would get more of the same, and that he wouldn't believe me anyway because

I was so bad. But he must have heard her shouting at me. He must have heard the sounds of physical abuse. But he did nothing. No doubt he was too scared of her to intervene – he knew full well the measure of her spite and anger against him whenever they rowed, which was often.

I could never do right by her. Presents I gave her weren't good enough. Attempts to please her, win her approval, fell on barren ground. I didn't look right. She told me that I was ugly, stupid, thick. I believed her. I took to hiding in the little shed or under a large flowering bush at the bottom of the garden; the scent of those flowers even now evokes that deadly, dragging ache of loneliness and fear.

And still no one knew. Neither family nor friends. No one knew at school why I was so awkward and why I never did well in exams. I kept up a front in order to protect her. And myself.

At eighteen I was pregnant and my mother wished me dead. Here again was evidence that I was disgusting and dirty, confirmed by the sister on the labour ward who treated me with utter contempt and echoed my mother's sentiment that it would be better if I were dead. When my son was born I loved him with every ounce of energy that I possessed; my mother could not bring herself to even touch him. Even he didn't seem to be good enough for her.

He deserved love and a secure, stable upbringing. I had all the love but I was told I could provide nothing else. I knew that I could not subject my beautiful son to possible abuse from my mother if I lived at home, and my own parenting would apparently be painfully inadequate. And so he was adopted – they took him from me twenty-two years ago and I was told I would not see him ever again unless he wanted to find me.

I kept the grief and guilt nailed down inside, unable to share it with a single soul.

Soon afterwards I left home, making a pathetic stab at being independent and self-sufficient. At least I was now out of her arm's reach. Needing physical comfort, needing to be held, however briefly, I based my relationships on sex. That was all that men seemed to expect of me, and I had no pride in myself or my body; I saw no reason to respect myself. By now I was desperately insecure and possessive – loss was just too unbearable to deal with, and I had no faith in myself or trust in anyone else.

Starting a nursing career, I struck on something of which my mother approved. My father began to open up to me, and when I passed my finals he was overjoyed and so proud of me. He and I had started to become friends for the first time.

When he died three months later, I somehow struggled on, battening down yet more pain and grief inside. I had known so little of him, but my mother refused to share any precious details with me.

A few years on, I was studying for a degree. I began to write letters to her, in an attempt to put our relationship on a new footing. We were adults – couldn't we start building something new...? Her gift to me when I graduated was a bookmark in the shape of a dagger.

She died eighteen months later, alone, and friendless. It was only then that I finally fell apart as the accumulated pain and exhaustion of the last thirty-four years welled up and spilled over. All those reasons for battling on through the years despite her cruelty were pointless now that she was dead.

In the last year I have sensed her presence in and around me like some malevolent miasma, pouring into my dreams, suffocating my spirit and threatening to engulf and annihilate me. How dare I finally explode the secrecy?! How dare I start to feel happy, confident, loved, worthwhile?! How dare I escape her stronghold?!

My Mother was a Footballer:
the Truth and Everything But

Rosa Ainley

She said: What is my mother? Is she the hardness in my chest, the line of my jaw and the wet in my eye? The fire in my head and the set of my shoulders?

I never dreamed about her, never thought she'd come back, never imagined I'd seen her, when I was a small girl who'd 'lost' my mother. 'Do you think I left her in the supermarket?' I wanted to say to all those people who couldn't say 'dead'.

Twenty years later I travelled to a country where my mother's family came from, or near enough. And I found her, on a train. Dark-red, coarse wavy hair, very petite, dressed in something like ski pants and a pair of very fetching decorated slippers, drop earrings and deep faraway eyes. I was too young to have known my mother red-headed, but this woman corresponded to an idea I never knew I had. I wished I spoke the language.

She said: I'll never know what it would've felt like but I know how much you loved me.

My mother had had trousers like that and those earrings, and I myself had a very similar pair of shoes. Genetic taste: all of which could only mean one thing. But how had she found out which train the daughter-she-hadn't-seen-for-so-long would be on? Well, information and foreigners in those countries, you know. Those mournful eyes, just waiting for Me, thin brown-haired version, to say: Mama!

Imagine the headlines:

> Hi Mum! 20 years later
> Family cruelly separated—Long Lost Mother
> KGB part in London family destruction: official
> NHS mix-up in dead mother shock
> Strangers on a train: me and my Mum

She said: So this is fiction? Damn you, why isn't my experience enough?

My experience? Death is the most isolating thing I've experienced in my life. Common as muck and natural as breathing. You're special, and is it catching? I still sometimes want to tell big, outrageous, fluorescent lies, talk fiction. A seriously expurgated version: truths acceptable for display. Not that I'd try to pretend it was easy, just that it was my imagination rather than my reality. Because I didn't want to think about it, and didn't want to admit how it feels when I do think about it. I didn't want to be embarrassed (or embarrassing), too exposing, too raw. I wasn't going to mythologise her, just run off—on paper anyway—and pretend it was about someone else. It was all about my mother, not me, and who was she anyway?

My mother was a doctor, and a couldabin... anything else she chose apparently—lawyer, journalist, footballer. So after she 'lost' my dad at the supermarket (and there's another story), she applied for transfer east. Maybe she just wanted to feel at home again after all that moving around: three continents in three generations, phew, permanent jet lag of the personality. Maybe she'd had it with suitable achievements for Jewish girls like gynaecology, and thought football incongruous enough.

Of course her game suffered, they just don't play the same over there, and she never quite got to grips with the different league structure. Then one night, travelling home from a fixture in western parts (god why do we have to go on these crowded tourist trains) she saw the smallest one, the one who didn't have red hair. Having difficulty with the language after so long, she heard, 'Sowherethefuckuvyoubeen?'

She said: She has been my unholy grail, the love of my life that I never had, the ultimate unrequited love.

I made my first mistake about half an hour after I knew you'd died. What was I to do? What would have made it better? Now, I'd cover the windows in black, and wail and cry, to well beyond the point when I'd look dead myself, accompanying myself with loud music. I'd immerse myself in tears and hold my breath, force myself under when I came up for air, until I felt my ears would burst. Now, I'd lie back and luxuriate in it, give myself enough rope. I'd suspend normal relations with all parties except the stereo and the vodka bottle, with occasional time out for serious cuddling, until I knew and understood and felt that you were, in your absolute absence, always there.

What I did instead was choose to escape the embarrassment of a dead mother and plenty of emotion that no one knows how to deal with, (children too, oh poor babies) and go downstairs. Where I knew people would not talk about It, would pat me until I stopped crying. Not long. I must have imagined kudos from this—for how else could I have learned it so quickly and thoroughly—but it was surely Relief On All Sides.

She said: Every hurt, every loss, is her too.
Someone else said, twenty years later: Cry now, or every loss is her again.

Later on that night I swallowed the sleeping pill. One brother put up resistance at this point: whether due to adolescent temperament or desire to experience fully pain of death of loved one remains uncertain. I don't remember waking up the next morning with the awful certainty of It's True shrieking in my head, probably because I didn't. I went to school.

And so it went on. I continued to allow occasional comforting patting until I stopped crying. Attempts at anything approaching real sympathy brought forth large sulks and bared teeth, but in any case this didn't happen often. Expressions of condolence I just didn't hear (thinking, I don't give a shit if you're *sorry* she's dead).

Everything changed and we were surrounded by people who kept up a pretence that it was all the same and Did Their Best. They didn't like it when I gave in and cried in corners because my mum was dead, or when I said the dreaded 'I want my mum' in the middle of crying over a cut knee. But then who would?

I still want my mum when I cut my knee, can't find a job, feel lost, break up with my lover, have flu, can't make a decision.

She said: Hey Ma, I feel like you only just left, often.

At school I mothered other girls whose mothers died because then I could mourn too. I pretended I understood: I'd been through it, and look at me, I was fine. At some point, the awful, often hidden shame of a dead mother transformed into the equally dangerous, but at least slightly glamorous notion of independence. A liberated parent-free existence—an outlook much encouraged by myself and my siblings of course.

She said (often): At least we had each other.
She said (often): Well, hey, at least she was around that long. (Eight years is enough for anyone isn't it?)

So from having no one, or not the genuine article, to come to parents' day and knit my jumpers, the scene shifted dramatically to the glory of being allowed to stay out late, and not being told off. It was exciting, romantic, tragic but we had been brave and were beyond it now.

She said: You will always disappoint. They want to be your mother, or they marvel at your strength because you can do without one.

I was left out again when my friends started getting on with their parents. After having nothing to rebel against as a teenager I now didn't have a girl's best friend, who'd read recipes out over the phone, make curtains, buy useful household items. All those girls' magazines that constantly advised, 'Ask your mum' about 'problems' from buying your first bra to thinking you're pregnant... I never needed a bra and I never got pregnant, but I wanted my mum within asking distance. I wanted a kind of 'How to...' guide, to Life in general (all that advice I'd missed out on that I could have ignored completely).

These images of Mother, of which my dreams were made, are someone else's mother, or no one's. Not simply an indication of how pernicious these Cornflakes-box representations are, they shout out my desire to fit it at all costs, particularly when I was well aware of their serious undesirability for a mother of mine and women in general. That's always been something both scary and shaming to me. The pride I felt about her difference had always been mixed with embarrassment. I had been different enough with a live mother—a dead one was too much. Rather than missing what she actually might have given me, I focused on missing these slight, but tangible goodies I saw being bestowed, or withheld, around me.

She said: Always jealous of anyone else having a mother, there is nothing I guard more jealously than my memory of you.

What I know about her life is very little, and I didn't know much about her death either. I lacked information at the time: I didn't know you were going to die, I didn't know what you died of until much later, or that you'd been cremated in Golders Green cemetery. I had this vague fantasy that you'd been disposed of in the hospital where you died. I imagined, what? A big oven (sick sick) in some subterranean corridor? a vast compost heap? a hospital-sized garbage masher truck? I didn't know I didn't know. I was told you were tired and in the strangeness, death from fatigue didn't seem out of place. There were times when, arriving at visiting time, only the adults were allowed in ('She's too tired and you're too noisy'). Damn them for their selfish and considerate protection. There was no preparation, no saying good-bye. To me it was quick and sudden, but your reality included knowing you had cancer (Q: For how long?), refusing surgery for a long time (Q: Why?), going into hospital eventually (Q: To die, or to try and recover?), operations (Q: How many, and what for?), quite a slow death really (Q: And a painful one?)

No one told me you were dying when I bought you a Christmas present in 1968. (I saw it all on screen in the film *My Life as a Dog*, and cried and cried, appalled at seeing in this way what had happened to me, but also pathetically grateful for this cultural confirmation of my experience.) What do you buy for the woman who has everything and is dying? I don't even know what date you died on. I didn't know I didn't know.

'She was so tired, she wanted to stay with you, but she was so very tired.' So couldn't she have had a good sleep then?

I wanted her to be there but I've also wanted her to know me, who I am and what I do and what I like. I never even had her to come out to. I've missed the benefit of her experience and the knowledge of my history as much as the security of her presence. If I knew all I need to about her death and about her life, I'd be learning more about myself too, who I am and where I come from. There's no one to ask, and even when it seemed like there was, they couldn't tell me. Maybe for the same reasons no one told me she was dying. If she'd been here my life would also have been materially much easier, but who would I have been then?

Surely everything but everything would have been completely different, in every way I can imagine, and no doubt, many that I never have. Her death, and the changes that followed, left me feeling always out of place, outside, out of focus, out on a limb, out out out; and is it in spite of her death or because of it that I'm also ferociously, and, I'm told, formidably certain of who I am and what I want to be (and it was never a gynaecologist or a footballer) as well as lost, vulnerable, uncertain? Sometimes almost simultaneously; it's hard work when you feel like an irreconcilable difference.

Twenty years I spent convincing anyone who was interested that it was kind of hard BUT it didn't affect anything, and some years since thinking I'll never get over it, being an eight-year-old who left her mother in the supermarket. It took another death, another unwanted house removal and other assorted losses before I caught up with it all, or rather it caught up with me. Talk about a heavy hand on the shoulder.

When someone dies you have to cross them out of your address book. Don't you? I can cross them out, eventually, but I can't remove the pages. I'm used to people being dead, I'm even used to them dying, but I don't stop wanting to ring them, sometimes.

She said: I'm a lesbian, and I wear my mother's wedding ring, proud as my life, and of hers.

Memories are notoriously inconsistent—after the sharpness of the picture and sound quality of being told my mum had died, deterioration sets in, so that anything else I remember has a muffled quality about it. I believe 'something died in me too' is the cliché most often employed in these situations, and quite a useful one it is too. I lived at some distance from myself after she died, and returned equipped with a full set of armour. I thought it made me safe, guarding the horror within, that if revealed no one would want to know, so nobody got to look. It was like wearing layers and layers of padding, and when I finally had to look I saw that I was very thin and eight years old.

She died   she left me   she didn't love me enough. All anyone really leaves you when they die is yourself. And if you get that much you should be grateful. I put on clothes that she might have worn, try on new glasses that turn me back into her. I worry what it means to be recreating her, but it's also a kind of security when she stares back from my mirror, looks through my wardrobe, uses my kitchen. And it looks good.

There's no escape you know, not even the fearful, almost-hopefulness of: Please don't leave me please love me forever please don't go. Ghost in my machine.

She said: Before I can forget I have to remember properly. I wish this could all be fiction, it's so hard it hurts me so much.

I wish you could have been there wish you could wish you were here had been here wish you could have been here wish you were here wish you could

Of Grief

May Sarton

Y ou thought it heartless
When my father fell down
Dead in his splendid prime,
Strong as a green oak thrown,
That all I did was praise
Death for this kindness,
Sang with a voice unbroken
Of the dear scholar's days,
His passion of a lifetime
And my loss never spoken.

Judge of another's grief?
Weigh out that grief in tears?
I did not weep my father,
The rich, the fulfilled years.
What slow death have you known?
When no hope or belief
Can help, no loving care?
We watch and weep alone.
My heart broke for my mother.
I buried grief with her.

It is the incomplete,
The unfulfilled, the torn
That haunts our nights and days
And keeps us hunger-born.
Grief spills from our eyes,
Unwelcome, indiscreet,
As if sprung from a fault
As rivers seam a rock
And break through under shock.
We are shaken by guilt.

There are some griefs so loud
They could bring down the sky,
And there are griefs so still
No one knows how deep they lie,
Endured, never expended.
There are old griefs so proud
They never speak a word;
They never can be mended.
And these nourish the will
And keep it iron-hard.

Charmian

Jill Posener

Eleven p.m. the phone rings. I'm relaxed, reading yesterday's paper. It's Bank Holiday Monday today, August 27th 1990, a day full of the attention of close friends trying to take my mind off my lover Susie who just left to return to our home in San Francisco. I'm in bed, the evening has been balmy and I'm engulfed in a delicious cosy haze, not alcohol-induced, though it feels a little like that.

I don't worry at the phone ringing. Reach out lazily. 'Hello Jill, it's Norman. Coates.' After sixteen years of marriage to my mum, Norman still introduces himself formally. What happened? It's not his tone of voice, which remains the same steady timbre throughout the next few days. It's 11 o'clock at night. That's why I feel a zipper running up the length of my body. What happened? My jaw stiffens, nothing like the quivering I feel very soon. He's trying to be calm, not to panic me, but to tell me something that doesn't want to come out of his mouth. Finally he says, in a dull voice, 'She may not live through the night.'

I'm 250 miles away. I have to be with my mum. Can I borrow a car and get there in time? Is there a night train? Flying, magic carpet, out-of-body transportation? I have to be with my mum. I can't work out what to do first, my brain seems to have every wire crossed. I tell Norman I'll call the boys then I'll call him back. Is he sure? How can she be dying? When I spoke to her on Saturday, she sounded stronger than at any time since her surgery a year ago.

Months later people will smile at me knowingly, nodding their heads with pity and amazement that I missed this obvious clue to her imminent death. And a year later, when I see *La Traviata* at the San Francisco Opera House I chuckle through my tears as the heroine rises from her deathbed with more energy than at any time in the opera, to sing her final aria and collapse into her lover's arms.

But on that Saturday, my mum's voice had leapt.

'Oh, darling, it'll be wonderful to see you,' she'd breathed in that tobacco-lung-cancer-surgically-scarred voice.

I phone my younger brother Ben, who's his usual sceptical self. Oh, Norman exaggerates. Hadn't we been told just two weeks earlier that we had at least six months with her? Ben wants to phone the hospital. I give him the number and the ward and the nurse on duty. He's in Berlin, as are my older brother Alan and my dad. Just two weeks ago we had all stood around my mum's bed, the gathering of the Poseners in a little village in Cleveland, and toasted her, honoured her, made peace with her, even made a little fun with her. Hours after her death, I asked her best friend: 'Was she happy, Lisa, after our visit?' 'She was happy as a pig in shit, Jill.' I liked that.

It's 11.10 p.m. The phone rings again. There's a howling, a devastating wailing on the other end and I feel myself falling against the white wall in the living room. I push against it to stay upright, the zipper unravels, my guts are spilling on the floor. She's dead, she's dead. I have never before heard Ben's agony. It's not like words anymore, we just stumble around sounds and howls. I'm not sure either of us is even standing anymore, but have we ever been so near to each other? Does Norman know, what do we do about Alan, the eldest of this trilogy of children? One thing is certain: we mustn't tell Dad tonight. He said when we visited my mum that when a man marries a woman twenty-three years his junior he doesn't expect to outlive her.

Norman's phone is busy. Three of us are trying to speak to one another, and the phones are busy. Later I phone the nurse myself. Tell me, was it peaceful, was she struggling? She reassures me that my mother simply said she was so tired, and then she just fell asleep. Why then, later, when I was screaming in the mortuary chapel of rest, were my mother's eyes open, glassy and staring, as though rest were the last thing on her mind?

I call my friend Sharon back. Don't worry about finding a train that runs tonight. She's dead. But I have to be with my mum. The first train leaves Kings Cross at 6 a.m. Every time I try to wrap myself in the comfort of my bedclothes and in the comfort of sleep, I'm tormented. I have to be with her. I worry she'll be cold by the time I get there. Often over the next few days I just want to climb onto the trolley with her body. Sharon spends the night. I can't be touched. I get up and wander to the toilet to grab handfuls of paper every few minutes, until Sharon suggests, gently, that I should bring the box of Kleenex into the bedroom.

The first sign that this is a farce as well as a tragedy comes in the morning, when there are no tubes or buses running that early to King's Cross and I can't get a taxi. On the train, tears dribbling down my cheeks, I don't care about the inquisitive faces, I don't bloody care.

9 a.m. The train arrives in Darlington. Norman is late. I try to imagine my mum leaving and arriving at this train station on her trips to London. As I try to use the loo and have to find the coins to put in the slot, I think, 'What a bar-

baric country, that makes people pay before you can even open the door to the stall.' I sob as I imagine my mum trying to use these. She would inevitably have carried the right change, her weak bladder had been a struggle all her life. My memories are full of Mum, in horrible discomfort, rushing to the nearest loo. She had laughed and cried in equal parts over that part of her anatomy.

The old red car arrives. Monty, a big German shepherd barking in the echoing halls of the station, then in the back, slobbering over the seat of the car. I think of my mum in the passenger seat of this scruffy car. Is this what it will be like? Every step, every moment a heart-wrenching memory? Norman sees my face, and just for a second scrunches his face up in pain. We don't touch, don't hug, the affection between us not easy, but there is a still and knowing bond between the two unlikely people in the car. He had been in many ways the traditional stepfather, aloof, afraid and engaged in a power struggle over the emotional terrain around my mother.

We drive in silence to the hospital. The nurses are tender. My mum would have hated the caretaking. They give us coffee. While we wait, I ask Norman to show me the room in which she died. It is the first of many acts for which I will be grateful later, but which seem, at the time, cruel and self-punishing. Like scratching an open wound, because the pain is somehow satisfying. A clue to being alive.

Two young nurses and a hospital porter (perhaps he wheeled her body last night to the mortuary) who is whistling happily through the corridors, walk with us to the mortuary. I feel a mixture of annoyance and relief at his thoughtlessness. I am clutching a bunch of her favourite flowers, beautifully pungent freesias. I had never visited my mum without them. I wasn't about to start now.

In the gloomy Chapel of Rest, lit a little like a photographic studio, there's a terrible spotlight on my mother's face. She looks like a seventeenth-century Dutch painting of an old woman, skin stretched like parchment across angular features, just her face showing above the wrapping. The wrapping is a pristine white linen sheet with a cross running down her chest. I run my fingers across her cheek, expecting her face to turn to me. I heave, run out screaming after the nurses, 'Why are her eyes open, why are her eyes open?' I can't evoke the sound of my screams: I've never heard anything like that come out of my throat before. They rush in, try to close the eyes and can't. Later in the week, when I see her in the funeral home, I torment myself with what they must have done to her to close her eyes and to make her look twenty years younger and as if she had fallen asleep in front of the telly.

The marvels of modern science. They couldn't keep her alive, but they could make her look magnificent in death.

Norman and I drive round the one-way town centre, make our way dismally to the Registrar of Births, Marriages and Deaths. Well, that is how it happens, isn't it? Life's phases as they happen, easily documented in one nondescript building in the centre of every town. Birth in Eastbourne, Marriage in Westminster (and again in Southend), Death in Middlesborough.

There's confetti on the staircase, one wedding in the front, as another moves out the back, there's newborn babes with underage parents looking absolutely out of control, and there's Norman and me. The Registrar adds my mum's name to the bound book on her oak desk. Elizabeth Charmian Coates, ne Middleton. Cause of death? She peers at the Death Certificate and my throat constricts again.

I leave Norman to complete the formalities, and wander into the nearest mall, and find a travel agent. I book my flight back to San Francisco.

Me, Norman and that barking dog drive back to the bungalow. This is my first sight of it since our visit two weeks ago when I had fallen to my knees in front of her and sobbed into her emaciated frame. 'Oh don't, Jill, please don't,' she had admonished me.

We walk through the gate, her nightdresses are hanging on the line, swaying in the breeze, swaying as she often did, a little unsteady on painful feet.

I wish they were unwashed. I want to inhale the tobacco and Tweed perfume smell that I always found too pungent in life. Norman begins the dismal task of finding a funeral director, and he keeps being distracted like a model train which keeps slipping off the tracks. I gently slip the front wheel back on the line, till it slips off again. I hear him stumbling on the phone as the salesman on the other end is trying to sell him a package he doesn't want. Over and over I hear him repeat: no pomp, no carnival, that's not what she wanted. No flowers, I hear Norman repeat for the fifth, the tenth time. 'If they can't bring me flowers when I'm alive, they'd better not do it when I die.' No pomp, no circumstance, it's not a bloody circus. To Norman's credit, he resists their elaborate plans. Mum would have been truly annoyed. I can hear her voice carrying the phlegm of disdain when she was irritated by stupidity, real or imagined. She hated the false politeness that seemed to be common in small town life. Yet she was dreadfully wounded by the petty gossips at the social club who brought about her fall as captain of the carpet bowls team.

In the end I persuade him to order one wreath of freesias. Freesias and my mum are stuck together in my memory of her, as firmly as the gin and cigarettes.

I, meanwhile, have been picking at my mum's belongings. When it is all over and months later I am wishing I had kept more clothing, just something to bury my face in, I will try and find motives for my haste. But on that day, that day when nothing really had to be done, on that day my work rate astonished even me. Perhaps I remembered my mum's reaction to her own mother's death. Chests of drawers tumbling on to the bed, clothes, shoes, make-up, bedclothes, jewellery, just thrown into suitcases, men arriving at the door to remove furniture. No time to waste. So here I was, sentimental, nostalgic me, working like a fury to clear up, clean up, and clear out.

I fold every item of clothing, I pack every new pullover and every skirt, even those she had had altered two weeks ago to fit her narrowing frame. I find the wig she bought after chemotherapy had begun to take its toll, and then the false teeth, and the spare sets. Throwing away her powder compact was the most painful thing I have ever done. The mirror in which she would have checked the evenness of the application, the groove worn into the powder. It was more intimate even than the satin lingerie, or the slippers with the imprint of her feet.

I get a cloth to clean up the bedside table; crumpled Kleenex and an overflowing ashtray are the last clues to my mother's recent residency.

I keep two sweaters, one for Ben, one for me. A week later I feel I have to wash it, the smell of my mother is overpowering. Now it sits in my wardrobe, unworn and no longer smelling of her. How silly to wish I'd done it differently. But when granny died in Wimbledon hospital in 1969, Mum had been ruthless. Later I often asked her for mementos, for photos, or the cigarette card collection I remember granny owning; she'd just retort 'I left in a hurry, darling. You forget.' Why had she left in such a hurry, I wondered. But that certainly had been a pattern, her 'leaving in a hurry' became both family joke and family paranoia. I used to make light of her absence from my life, but my months in the bedsit alone in my final year of school left me bitter and confused. She always returned, the schemes or the men somehow a disappointment, neither the men nor the schemes they were meant to be.

And as I hurriedly pack her things, as though she has a plane to catch, I'm aware that my mum left in a hurry yet again, without really saying goodbye.

But in her way, she had said it perfectly adequately. We stood round her bed, and each one in turn had our private talk. During that visit, I had asked some prying questions, looking for truth. And like the slap in the face I always got for cheek, the answer came in the form of brutal directness. 'You always irritated me, Jill, you were never the daughter I wanted.' Just as I remembered. I had been in love with my mother for so long as a child. I had watched her dress for an evening out, had observed the rituals of a woman preparing herself for being admired. I'd sat in a corner and felt the silk on her skin, and smelt the scent and the hairspray. I'd leapt from the chair to fasten her zipper at the back of a tight dress revealing perfect brown shoulders. And often, after my parents had left for the evening, I'd masturbated on their bed. It wasn't my mother, exactly, but a woman in a tight dress and smelling of make-up and hairspray who filled my head.

And when the clothes were gone, to be recycled at the local hospital, and the bed was cleaned, as I took the billowing clothes from the line, I wanted only to be able to bury my head in her crotch, when her strong arms around my head meant that everything was right with the world. I grew with her hard words ringing in my ears, but filled with the certainty of her protective love. When I was no longer a child but, in her mind at least, a teenage competitor, the affair was over, but, unlike all the following love affairs, this one and its failure tormented me.

As we sent my mum in her tiny coffin into the oven I sat with this family of boys and felt like a succeeding matriarch. I wondered why it was necessary for six men to carry the coffin. She weighed next to nothing when she died. I remembered the funeral charges, and the bill said six bearers and that, I suppose, is that.

After the funeral, people would silently approach us, this family of foreigners in an English village. Leaning in towards me conspiratorially, they told me how I resembled my mother.

I had spent my lesbian adulthood avoiding that very thing. My passionately, determinedly heterosexual mother, with her secret love affairs, the broken hearts and crushed egos behind her. I'd thought it much more romantic to see myself in my paternal grandmother, Gertrude Oppenheim, Jewish, long dead, no chance to disapprove of me. But suddenly, I could see the beauty in my mother's piercing eyes, the roundness of her cheeks, the baby-like hair, flying away like wisps of smoke.

Elizabeth Charmian Middleton was born on the 6th March 1928 in Eastbourne and spent a childhood on the south coast of England. Desperate for adventure she married a much older man and, to the dismay of her proper English mother, a German Jew. Charmian and Julius Posener were married in 1948 in the Registry Office in Westminster. She spent a confused married life in London, Kuala Lumpur and Berlin, before escaping back to her mum and a love affair with another even older German in 1965. She was a drinker, a smoker, a flirt and prankster. She wrote stories and told a few. She found men irresistible and the feeling was clearly mutual. Her common-law husband, Sophron, died in 1972 and her second marriage, to Norman, remained intact and happy until her death.

My mum kept a diary between the years 1955 and 1959,

sealed with strict instructions that it was not to be read until after her death. In it I read of a tangled love affair, about the pain of loving two men simultaneously, about her determination to have the affair and to remain in her marriage. I read that I had been a happy child, a lively gorgeous dancer, and that she had adored me. Finally allowing her anger and her cruelties to be balanced by these revelations, I discovered a love that I had all but concealed in the bottom of a closet. A love for my mother and, more importantly, for myself.

One Pushed, One Pulled, Three Nurtured

Shirley P. Cooper

I suppose everyone had had their signs. Dogs barking, doors knocking, dreams about teeth. My little sister Medora who was only a few months old when Uvina died had been crying out in her sleep nights before for her Mama Vina. When the news of her death came I remember wondering why my big sister was crying so for her mama. My mama was in the yard with me. But Frances was distraught. I was playing in the corner of the yard when a very tall man came to the gate and shouted, 'Miss Clarke, you is the woman who have Uvina children? Well, they find her dead in her room.' Uvina was rumoured to have committed suicide after killing her boyfriend. This was near Christmas 1958.

She conceived me and carried me for nine months. I was Uvina Cooper's second daughter. Uvina was the daughter of George E. Cooper, the auctioneer. He also made mattresses and belts: I remember climbing on top of the mattresses when I was little. When Uvina was young he left her in St Kitts and took the rest of the family to Trinidad. That's how she came to live in Baker's Corner with Miss Clarke and started calling her Mama. Anyway when my mother started labour my father was sent to get the midwife. I was a few weeks old by the time he came back again, and by that time Mama had taken over. She named me Shirley as I was born just after midnight Sunday. There was a big fight during the Christening. My father picked on my mother. My godmother joined in and then her friend said if Anguilla (my father) was fighting St Kitts (my mother), then Dominica (my god-mother) had to join in.

When I was three Uvina was sent to England by her father because 'she was just there having all these bastard children for these worthless men.' My grandfather disapproved of every suitor my mother had. One time he lifted up my mother to throw her out of the window because she'd made another bad choice. She was his only 'inside' daughter and she was forever shaming him. Life in those days was pretty hard for black people and she was very lonely. When I read her letters in 1972 and 1979 they brought tears to my eyes. She missed her children but she felt they were safe with Mama, poor but happy.

Mama lived till she was over seventy. She was a Dominican woman. Mr Clarke had gone to Dominica to work and had asked Johannah's mother for her. They moved back to St Kitts where up to her death Mama stayed a for-eigner. Mr Clarke died round about 1963. He was a hard-working man and although they had never had any children, they reared over twenty-two. I lived with her until I was three. She never had electricity in those days and she still lived in the yard in Baker's Corner. Mama managed on whatever the parents sent her, which was sometimes noth-ing. Mama didn't have a sewing machine, so when people sent her pieces of cloth to make clothes for their children, she couldn't always afford to give it out. Sometimes it was used for lodging; rolled up to make pillows placed on the floor to cushion us against the floorboards as we slept.

Every Christmas Eve we went window shopping. Most years Father Christmas managed to bring us all a balloon. The Roman Catholic Church which Mama went to had a fête every year. Mama would take us there and let us play with all the toys. We would push the push-along toys the full length of the floor all day and at the end Mama would buy us a balloon each and we'd go home happy. No one ever had a whole doll until Frances' father sent her a Cinderella doll from England. Mama kept it so we wouldn't mash it up. On special occasions, we would wash our hands, take it out and play with it for a while then put it away till next time.

When Mama shared out our food in the yard she used to tell us why we should eat it all up. I knew banana had iron in because those were the little black bits that made us strong, Mama said. She used to give us castor oil, Phospherene, Cod Liver Oil and Malt to make us grow, and put purple lotion and calamine on our cuts and bruises. If you were really lucky you'd get a plaster, but you'd quicker get dirt rubbed on it.

We went to Church and Sunday School every week. Mama would put ribbons in our hair, put shoes and socks on us and send or carry us to Church. We'd attend probably five times on Sunday and Bible Classes during the week. On special occasions she would dress us up and take us to get our picture taken 'for Mama Vina to see how big we get'.

When Mama Vina got a job in England, Papa came to take us to his big house. Mama protested that Mama Vina had given her instructions, but Papa had influential friends. Papa wanted me to go and live with Mrs Cranston because she was a widower and rich. She was our cousin, and used to come to comb our hair. She loved me because I was the prettiest with the fair skin and long hair.

Mama Vina wrote to Papa and told him to put her children back where she left them, at Mama's. Mama had instructions to take us under the boat if she wanted to. This was the local term for prostitution: it meant that Mama had Mama Vina's permission to do whatever she liked with us. We went back to King Street.

When Mama Vina died in 1958 Mrs Cranston took me to live with her.

She could provide me with all the material things Mama Clarke couldn't, they said. We lived in Dorset Village at first. I was supposed to go to a private school but I had turned up on the first day with the wrong hat. I went to a girls' school which was too much for Mummy to bear: when she got some money she was taking me out of there.

Mrs Cranston was a proud woman, and she chose her friends very carefully. She had travelled and owned houses in St Kitts. Every so often she gave me back to Mama Clarke and went to Aruba to help her daughter. But when the oil company laid off a lot of people, those without Dutch nationality had to leave for St Kitts or England. America didn't want any more West Indians. So her family headed for England. They sent home most of their furniture for Mrs Cranston, who sold it to Papa who said he needed it but within days it was auctioned. Mummy said Papa was a thief. He didn't give her much money for the furniture but he bought me a suitcase to go to England.

Then Mummy's daughter called for help. England was hard. Her last child had drunk some poison at a childminder's and nearly died. She needed her mother to childmind while she went to work. Her daughter had enough mouths to feed and didn't want me. Mummy didn't want to leave me this time. She was coming with me or not at all. They compromised. Mummy could bring me but she had to pay. Mummy read me the letter. We were going to England for a few months then returning to St Kitts. Mummy rented out the house in Thompson St – the bathpan, the piano, the radio, they all got packed up. Mama was at the airport. She reassured me that I was leaving one sister in St Kitts to meet another in England. We were going to Leeds 8 and my Sister lived one Leeds away. Leeds 7. I cried and screamed and had to be carried onto the aeroplane.

Southampton was smoky, cold and noisy on September 23rd 1963. At Customs they took the bottles of Alcalado and Bay Rum. Mummy told them to give it to their Queen as she wasn't paying duty for it. Mummy's daughter came to meet us. So this was the woman who mek me leave Mama and Medora and come England. We went by train to London. On the way Mummy put her suitcase on her head to carry it. Her daughter told her that in England nobody carries things on their heads. Mummy said they were stupid people then. The bus was full so we had to go upstairs. It didn't look full to me – they could have held more and more like them trucks back home. We went upstairs. There were loads of factories where we went with all the smoke coming out of the top. Then we stopped and put a key in a door. There was a family inside. I went out in the garden with the children and asked if I could have some apples off the tree. They laughed at my funny accent.

The next day we went to Leeds, where I met the rest of the family and all the other people living in the house. Mummy and I shared a room with Mrs Matthew, her daughter Patsy and grandchild. On September 27th I had my first birthday in England. I also had my first fight with one of my cousins.

During the day Mummy looked after a lot of children. The snow soon came and Mummy didn't have a coat. I got a big duffle coat and went to school. I hated it. I wanted to go back to St Kitts.

Soon Mrs Matthew moved out and we had the room to ourself. Mummy didn't like living there: she wanted to help her daughter but she didn't like the way we were treated. One day she asked one of her grandchildren to bring down the heater for her as usual so she could keep the children warm.

'Tell Shirley to do it. You prefer her to us.'

Mummy went up the stairs to get the heater and fell on the way down. She broke her leg and went to hospital. Our first Christmas found us huddled in a cold room. When Mummy's leg was better we were moving out. That Christmas I got a balaclava and I saw when Mummy's daughter put it by my bed.

One morning Mummy woke me up and we lay in bed having a long talk. When we'd finished she told me to go and get her daughter. The ambulance came and took her away. I never saw her again. She died of pneumonia on February 23rd. I cried alone at first. The day of the funeral I wore a purple satin dress with pleated skirt. When we got back I turned on the radio and Mummy's daughter found me dancing to the music. She cursed me and blamed me for her mother's death. I cried and screamed for days. Eventually they called in a doctor. He called in another one who called in another one. I was finally injected to calm me down. I don't remember what happened next. Mama reminded me in 1972 and 1978 when she gave me all my mother's letters and all those I had written from 1963 onwards that I took a vow of silence after that. I wasn't loving anyone else. Everyone I'd loved so far had died. I wrote Papa and asked him to send for me. He couldn't afford it he said. He told Mama 'in England when you don't have anybody the government look after you.' In St Kitts he would have had to. I carried on writing to him but I kept it impersonal. The letters to Mama always left tear-stained and as I used to write with a fountain pen she could hardly read them.

Sometimes the replies were opened. I started addressing

them next door as we lived at 11a and next door was 11. After reading, I would tear them up. Life after Mummy's death was awful. I called myself Shirleyella as per Cinderella. I read *Jane Eyre* from cover to cover on numerous occasions. I started reading *Bunty*, *Judy* and *Mandy*, especially the awful stepmother stories. I did very well at school. Mummy and Mama had given me a good start. I lived on memories. I made decisions about my life.

Nine years to the day when I'd arrived I left Leeds. I went to college to prove to everyone that no matter what they did to me I was going to be somebody. I had cried a lot that year.

I've been luckier than most. I've had three mothers. Uvina, Mama, Mummy. Now Mama was the only one left of the three. Christmas 1972 I went back to St Kitts to cry on her shoulder. I stayed in her house, with no electricity, flushing toilet or running water. She had two children with her. I saw how much she'd done for us. Those children were still treated to a balloon on special occasions. She gave them the last piece of bread and went without. She could hardly look after herself but the children lived on love and bits brought by the neighbours. One day when everyone was out Mama gave me a bundle of letters to read. She'd kept all mine and Mama Vina's. She gave me her chain and wedding ring. I came back to England and carried on writing to her.

When I made another trip to St Kitts in 1978 Mama's living conditions had got worse. She was still referred to as the Dominican woman but now she had another title: The Obeah woman. Children teased her. When I went to see about getting the children taken into care and Mama in a Home I was told in no uncertain terms, 'Lady this ain' England with they Social Services.'

The boy's father wanted me to pay him to keep the child.

Their mother never replied when I wrote. So I took them to a relative in the country. Mama was heartbroken.

In 1980 whilst I was pregnant I came home one day and found a letter on the mat. I looked at it and burst into tears. I rushed out of the house grasping my letter. I went up the road to a friend's but her daughter told me she'd gone out. I crossed the road not knowing where I was going with the tears streaming down my face. Then someone called me back: her mum was in. She'd thought it was the Insurance man. She was very sympathetic. I showed her the letter and told her that Mama was dead. 'But you haven't opened it.'

'I know she's dead.' I finally opened the letter. Mama was dead. The child inside me kicked even more than usual. I named my daughter Johannah after her. When she went to work in St Kitts the white master said he didn't like her name and called her Josephine. I gave it back to her in 1978.

To me a mother is someone who loves and looks after you, so boyfriends' mothers become mine and remain so even when our relationship is over. Every Mother's Day I send cards to mothers – my ex's and others who have been good to me. Most people have one mother. This is a tribute to three of mine. I have had a lot more since them.

Signing On and Signing Off

Frances Kenton

My invisible ball and chain tug.
I am unemployed,
Time to Sign On.

I leave my mother and phone:
'There is serious illness in the family.
I cannot come.'

'You must.
Just to sign your name,
To make it plain you are not in work.'

Weary I ride to town
And sign.

Hospital again,
Obese with technology,
Famous for its addiction to transplants.
I have a Donor Card in every pocket.
Forgotten, they are washed – frequently.

My unseen cord tugs me to Ward Four.
My mother's vague resemblance is still there,
Still restless, overheated inwardly,
Worn heart jerked automatically,
Her bed a tapestry of plumbing.
I concentrate on shapes within the spaces.
Nearly time, I think, for her to Sign Off.

Cardiograph mountains crumble.

They tell me right-sided heart failure is rare,
Is interesting. They could learn so much.

I sign
Away her body.

'My mother wanted to donate her eyes.'

I sign
Away her eyes.

Invisible, my mother comes with me out of the
hospital.

Unspoken Thoughts

Moira McLean

This vigil. Day after day we sit like bolsters and observe your untreatable heart and kidney failure. Horrifically your mind clears as you physically disintegrate. You accuse and torture us. On and on and on. I will you to die. Quickly. You are killing my father who sits in his loose skin frantic with fear, guilt and sorrow. Clumsily he tries to comfort. You pull your hand away, turn your head. I hate you.

Then the well-known euphemism, 'There is a spare side ward for your mother. It will be quieter, more private.'

I reassure your nagging with pretence.

Don't die. I love you... but YOU taught me to paper the cracks. YOU taught me to play Happy Families so well. YOU taught me to bury reality if it was not acceptable – at whatever cost. I hate you. So I pretend real death is not happening. I lie... and love... and hate... until you become extinct.

Planning a Funeral

A funeral doesn't have to be the awesome, inappropriate, embarrassing experience described by some of the writers in this anthology. Nor does it have to be an event that you eternally wish had been done differently. The following pages outline practical details of what must be done to organise a funeral, and also ideas for some alternatives to the standard practice.

A funeral is an important way of marking a major event in your life, not only as a recognition of the end of a life, but also the beginning of life without that person. The marking of death and expression of grief form an essential part in the process of grieving. A funeral may provide comfort after the death of someone loved and close; it may bring confirmation of an unbelievable event – the beginning of acceptance that death has happened. The responsibility for organising a funeral may be a welcome distraction from thinking about the person who has just died or it can seem like the heaviest and most cruel burden that a recently-bereaved person has to shoulder.

Depending on how close the dead person was to you (and how liberal your employer regarding compassionate leave) you will probably be allowed time off work, at least to attend the funeral. Funerals can be particularly difficult for lesbians and gay men: however close they may have been to the dead person, lover or friend, they may be unable to approach the biological family, or may be deliberately or tacitly excluded from proceedings. It may also be impossible to explain why time off work is needed, or it may not be seen as a good enough reason.

It's very common to hear people referring to the time just after a funeral as when the death really sank in, and grief became overwhelming. Many see this as a benefit – that the necessity of arranging a funeral can often, for that initial period, overtake anything else, including numbing over-powering feelings of grief. Of course, it's not certain that this is anything to do with the funeral – it's just as likely that the feelings of shock and disbelief following a death have begun to wear off.

The next-of-kin, or carer, will be given the death certificate stating the cause of death, which you need before attempting to plan the funeral. Assuming there are no special circumstances such as a *post mortem* (this happens when there is reason to believe that death was not due to natural causes) or an inquest (necessary in cases of sudden or unexplained death), you are free to concentrate on deciding what kind of funeral you want to organise.

Some people leave very specific instructions about their own funeral, including information such as whether they want to be cremated or buried, lists of whom to invite, where to hold it, music to listen to, food to provide. There's no legal obligation to carry out the wishes expressed by the dead person regarding the funeral, although it is usual practice. There are endless reasons why the executor or next of kin may choose to ignore these wishes; the cost of the funeral is usually paid out of the deceased's estate (money and property left) and there may not be enough money to provide whatever the request is, or it may be something too difficult to arrange or too painful. If no instructions have been left, it is up to you, as a sole or group responsibility, to make decisions about what kind of occasion it will be.

Although the majority of people in this country are not practising Anglicans, most people choose the regular service offered by the local undertakers. This will be a Church of England ceremony, with prayers, hymns and a short sermon by a minister who will probably make an effort to come and talk to the dead person's family and/or friends before the funeral, if they are not part of his or her regular congregation, followed by a burial or cremation. If the body is to be cremated rather than buried you will also need a cremation certificate, signed by two doctors, and for which you must pay (at time of publication the cost was £26.50). The death must be registered within five days at the local Registry Office, but it isn't necessary to do this before contacting a funeral parlour. A religious ceremony, of whatever denomination, can be organised through any funeral director, who would also help in finding a suitable minister if you did not already have someone in mind.

Each religious community has its own funeral organisations, but at most cemeteries any type of religious (or non-religious) service may be held. Expense should be discussed with the funeral director: dying can be an expensive business and it's important to be aware of cost and to avoid being railroaded into something more expensive than you had intended.

It's clear from the stories in *Death of a Mother* that children, given clear information, are well equipped to grieve, and indeed often try to protect adults from having to deal with their – the children's – grief as well as their own. So if there are children involved, they should be told about what is going to happen and asked if they want to come to the funeral.

Press announcements, if made, in local and national papers should include details of the funeral, whether or not it is private, whether there is also going to be a memorial service, whether flowers or donations are requested and where they should be sent.

There are other options. A celebration organised yourself will, by its nature, be very personal. A funeral is, after all, the last service you can offer to someone you have been close to, whatever the relationship. You may want to choose particular songs and readings, special flowers, and you have to decide on the type of coffin for the body to be placed in and whether it will be in place before the mourners arrive or whether it will be brought in as they enter. You have to think about the kind of occasion you want, and what the dead person would have wanted. A grand event or a quiet gathering? A noisy celebration of life or a place for people to be able to express their grief?

You may decide to take the service yourself, as an individual or a group, talking about the dead person or reading from something they liked or that seems appropriate to you, or you may prefer to make it an open participation funeral where any of the people present can read a story or poem, or speak about the dead person. It may be true that many non-believers have religious funerals because it's easier to accept what is immediately on offer, and also that it may seem like much more – too much – effort is required to organise any alternative.

If there is no one available to officiate at the funeral (and during a time of bereavement the confidence and organisational skill necessary may well be in short supply), the British Humanist Association or the National Secular Society (addresses overleaf) will offer advice and try to supply an officiant to take the ceremony. Cost for this service should be worked out with the organisation. Whoever is in charge of the ceremony must make sure that those present are told at the beginning how the ceremony works. It is also possible to add a 'personal' section to a Church of England service, where friends and colleagues perform a second service more in keeping with the beliefs of the deceased.

Whatever you decide, at the end of the ceremony comes the committal, to the ground in the case of burial, or to the crematorium; this is likely to be the most upsetting part of the occasion. You can choose to leave the committal until everyone has gone, but bear in mind that this poses its own problems and that deferring distress may not make it any less. After a cremation you can keep the ashes or scatter them somewhere you choose, or leave them to be disposed of by the crematorium. You may want to have somewhere to go and 'visit'. Of course this does not have to be the place where the coffin was put or where the ashes were scattered: it could be a part of your home, or in your garden, or some place that meant something between you.

After the ceremony you may want to have some kind of reception or wake or party. Again decisions need to be made: someone's house or a public place; what sort of food and drink; whether to leave it open-ended or have a set period of time. And finally, think about going home: do you want to be alone, or with people? Are you returning to the home you have shared with the person who is now dead, and if so, is that what you want? Having in mind what you are doing the next day, even if it's staying home and crying, is important too, so that you do not feel like the funeral is the end of everything. Whatever your own beliefs about what happens when people die, for you yourself the funeral is a marker that death has happened recently, however that leaves you feeling.

In late twentieth-century Britain, wearing mourning clothes or observing a period of mourning are generally seen as old-fashioned and unnecessary. Even talking about the dead person too much tends to be frowned upon as evidence of 'not getting over' the death or of wallowing in an unhealthy fashion. The need for rituals is mentioned by several of the contributors – lighting candles, revisiting old haunts, covering mirrors, wearing special jewellery and clothes. These are ways to remember, ways to ensure never forgetting the dead person, of, perhaps, keeping them with you and simultaneously marking and accepting their absence. There are many religious rituals but you can either borrow or make up your own. Observing rituals is a way of allowing death into life as an extra/ordinary sad experience, rather than the funeral ending any public expression about the death, signifying the time to get over it and get on with living – an attitude that displays a marked ignorance about the processes of life.

British Humanist Association
14 Lamb's Conduit Passage
London WC1R 4RH
071–430 0908

National Secular Society
702 Holloway Road
London N19 3NL
071–272 1266

Booklist and Organisations

This list is not meant to be exhaustive. I've deliberately included a lot of fiction because so many women have said how helpful they found particular books. I've also purposely left out some 'classic' bereavement texts, for the opposite reason, and partly because they're easy to uncover.

Barbara Burford, *The Threshing Floor* (Sheba, 1986).

Kim Chernin, *In My Mother's House* (Virago, 1985).

Sandra Chick, *I never told her I loved her* (The Women's Press, 1989).

Simone de Beauvoir, *A Very Easy Death*, (Penguin, 1964).

'Death', *Granta* 27, Summer 1989.

Lucy Ellman, *Sweet Desserts* (Penguin, 1987).

Gary Glickman, *Years from Now* (Minerva, 1989 [out of print]).

Marilyn Hacker, 'Against Silence', in *Going Back to the River* (Random House, 1990).

John Hinton, *Dying* (Penguin, 1967).

Zora Neale Hurston, *Dust Tracks on a Road* (Virago, 1985).

—, *Their Eyes Were Watching God* (Virago, 1986).

Elisabeth Kübler-Ross, *On Death and Dying* (Tavistock, 1970).

—, *Death: The Final Stage of Growth* (Prentice-Hall, 1975).

C. S. Lewis, *A Grief Observed* (Faber & Faber, 1961).

Drusilla Modjeska, *Poppy* (Serpent's Tail, 1991).

Michael Ondaatje, *In the Skin of the Lion* (Picador, 1988).

Ann Scott, 'Joan Scott: Living Her Dying', *Spare Rib* 57, March 1977; also in Sue O'Sullivan (ed.), *Women's Health: A Spare Rib Reader* (Pandora, 1987).

What to do when someone dies (Consumers' Association—get the latest edition).

Organisations

Bereavement Counselling and Support

Cruse
126 Sheen Road
Richmond
Surrey TW9 1UR
081–940 4818

Gay Bereavement Project
Vaughan M. Williams Centre
Colindale Hospital
London NW9 5GH
081–200 0511

NAFSIYAT Intercultural Therapy Centre
278 Seven Sisters Road
London N4 2HY
071–263 4130

National Association of Bereavement Services
122 Whitechapel High Street
London E1 7PT
071–247 1080

National Association of Victim Support Schemes
Cranmer House
39 Brixton Road
London SW9
071–735 9166

Off Centre
Adolescents' Counselling Service
20 Hackney Grove
London E8 3NR
081–986 4016

Women's Therapy Centre
6 Manor Gardens
London N7
071–263 6200

Planning a Funeral

Humanist Association
14 Lamb's Conduit Passage
London WC1R 4RH
071–430 0908

National Secular Society
702 Holloway Road
London N19 3NL
071–272 1266

Can offer advice about organising non-religious funerals and will conduct ceremonies; the Humanist Association also produces a booklet called *Funerals Without God* (£3).

Of further interest...

MOTHERS WHO LEAVE

Behind the myth of women without their children

ROSIE JACKSON

In this new, compassionate approach to a controversial and complex subject, Rosie Jackson asks what can drive a mother to relinquish her children and examines the emotional aftermath. Exploding the myths that surround such mothers, she explores this dark side of mothering with unusual depth and sensitivity.

'Rosie Jackson's important new book is the first contemporary account and analysis of women who felt unable to stay in the primary parenting situation.'

SUSIE ORBACH, *THE GUARDIAN*

The Dance of Anger

Harriet G. Lerner

Do you find yourself always fighting with your nearest and dearest, distancing yourself though silence, or blaming others for the failure of your relationships?

For so many young women anger is a destructive force which perpetuates all the harmful dynamics of our most intimate relationships. In this classic, inspirational book, renowned feminist psychotherapist Harriet G. Lerner shows how all women, regardless of age, background or experience, can turn anger into a constructive force.

The Dance of Intimacy

Harriet G. Lerner

All intimate relationships can be terribly damaged by too much distance, too much intensity or simply too much pain.

In clear, direct and dramatic terms, Harriet G. Lerner illustrates how we can move differently in these key relationships—be they with a distant or unfaithful spouse, a depressed sister, a difficult mother, an uncommitted lover or a family member we have written off.

THE DANCE OF DECEPTION

HARRIET G. LERNER

Pretending, says Dr Lerner, is so closely associated with femininity that it is, quite simply, what our culture teaches women to do.

Going beyond conventional distinctions between deception and honesty, good and bad, this deeply humane book gives a penetrating analysis of what lying represents in a society where women's 'truths' are so often unspoken truths, as well as providing perceptive guidance for changing behaviour patterns which distort our real selves.

Harriet G. Lerner PhD is staff psychologist at the Menninger Clinic in the United States and an internationally renowned expert on the psychology of women.

When A Baby Dies

NANCY KOHNER AND ALIX HENLEY

This compassionate book offers insight and information for all parents whose babies have died, their families and friends, and professionals who care for them.

Every year thousands of babies die before birth or shortly afterwards. For the parents, the grief is hard to bear. In this book, parents who have lost a baby tell their stories. They speak about what happened, how they felt, how they have been helped by others and how they helped themselves.

Using letters from and interviews with many bereaved parents, Nancy Kohner and Alix Henley have written a book which offers understanding of what it means to lose a baby and the grief that follows. *When A Baby Dies* also contains valuable information about why a baby dies, hospital practices, the process of grieving, sources of support, and the care parents need in future pregnancies.

TOO DEEP FOR TEARS

SARAH BOSTON

In 1981, Sarah Boston published the award-winning *Will, My Son: The Life and Death of a Mongol Baby*, in which she told the story of the birth, the nine-month-long life and the death of her son Will, born with Down's Syndrome. The book served as an extraordinary catalyst to the debate about disability, maternal grief and medical practice, and became standard reading for practitioners as well as the many ordinary people who have gone through similar experiences.

Too Deep for Tears celebrates what should have been Will's eighteenth birthday. Written in the same searchingly honest and direct style, this unique document looks at what has and has not changed in the last two decades in society's attitudes towards Down's Syndrome, infant death and maternal grief. The author looks at the effect of the publication of *Will, My Son* on her and her family, at the couple who decided to adopt a Down's baby after reading it and the 'burden of preciousness' her daughter has carried, at current issues of ante-natal testing and medical practice and, crucially, at the longevity of grief.

'I read *Will, My Son* with profound respect—
and sadness—for Sarah Boston.'

DIRK BOGARDE

LOVE: A USER'S GUIDE

Intimacy from birth to death

JANE KNOWLES

As a psychiatrist and psychotherapist, Jane Knowles claims that about 80 per cent of her clients' problems stem from their need for, search for, and disappointment in love. *Love: A User's Guide* is a popular and comprehensive psychology book exploring the many forms this vexed emotion can take: parental, sexual, sibling, spiritual, friendship and so on, from a woman's point of view.

The author takes us on an illuminating journey through our emotional lives from the moment a newborn baby feels its first rush of love—and hate—for the Mother to the turbulent passions of adolescence and the flourishing sexuality of full adulthood right through to the calmer, mellower but equally rewarding friendships of old age. Accessible, well-written and entertaining, Knowles draws extensively on case histories and her professional experience.

MOTHERS WHO LEAVE	0 04 440899 4	£8.99	☐
THE DANCE OF ANGER	0 04 440866 8	£6.99	☐
THE DANCE OF INTIMACY	0 04 440865 X	£6.99	☐
THE DANCE OF DECEPTION	0 04 440931 1	£6.99	☐
WHEN A BABY DIES	0 04 440566 9	£6.99	☐
TOO DEEP FOR TEARS	0 04 440891 9	£6.99	☐
LOVE: A USER'S GUIDE	0 04 440855 2	£7.99	☐

All these books are available from your local bookseller or can be ordered direct from the publishers.

To order direct just tick the titles you want and fill in the form below:

Name: _____

Address: _____

_____

_____ Postcode: _____

Send to: Thorsons Mail Order, Dept 3, HarperCollins*Publishers*, Westerhill Road, Bishopbriggs, Glasgow G64 2QT.
Please enclose a cheque or postal order or your authority to debit your Visa/Access account—

Credit card no: _____

Expiry date: _____

Signature: _____

—to the value of the cover price plus:

UK & BFPO: Add £1.00 for the first book and 25p for each additional book ordered.

Overseas orders including Eire: Please add £2.95 service charge. Books will be sent by surface mail but quotes for airmail despatches will be given on request.

24 HOUR TELEPHONE ORDERING SERVICE FOR ACCESS/VISA CARDHOLDERS—TEL: **041 772 2281.**